DRACULA

THE GRAPHIC NOVEL
Bram Stoker

Based on a script by Jason Cobley

Australia • Brazil • Japan • Korea • Mexico • Singapore • Spain • United Kingdom • United States

Dracula: The Graphic Novel
Bram Stoker
Script By Jason Cobley

Publisher: Sherrise Roehr

Editor In Chief, Classical Comics: Clive Bryant

Development Editor: Cécile Engeln

Director of Product Marketing: Ellen Lees

Product Marketing Manager: Brian Romeo

Director of Content Production: Michael Burggren

Association Content Project Manager: Mark Rzeszutek

Production Intern: Carolina Jaramillo

Print Buyer: Mary Beth Hennebury

Linework: Staz Johnson

Coloring: James Offredi

Lettering: Jim Campbell

Design & Layout: Jo Wheeler & Carl Andrews

ISBN-13: 978-1-111-83849-2

ISBN-10: 1-111-83849-6

National Geographic Learning
20 Channel Center Street
Boston, MA 02210
USA

Cengage Learning is a leading provider of customized learning solutions with office locations around the globe, including Singapore, the United Kingdom, Australia, Mexico, Brazil, and Japan.

Visit National Geographic Learning online at **ngl.cengage.com**

Visit our corporate website at **www.cengage.com**

Printed in the United States of America
Print Number: 06   Print Year: 2022

Contents

DRACULA

Characters

Count Dracula

Jonathan Harker

Mina Murray / Harker
Jonathan's fiancée / wife

Lucy Westenra
Mina's friend

Arthur Holmwood
Lucy's fiancé

Dr. John "Jack" Seward
Arthur's friend

Quincey Morris
Arthur's friend

Renfield
Dr. Seward's patient

Dr. Abraham Van Helsing
Dr. Seward's friend

Prologue

This story was put together from journals and letters written by the people who were involved in the events.

CHAPTER ONE

Jonathan Harker's Journal

May 3

I left Munich on May 1st and arrived at Klausenburgh after dark.

There are four **nationalities** in Transylvania. I am going where the **Szekelys** live. They are **descended** from **Attila** and the **Huns**.

I did not sleep well. A dog howled all night under my window. I had to rush through my breakfast to catch the train. And then the train was late!

We traveled through the countryside all day.

It was nearly dark when we finally got to Bistritz, near the Borgo Pass.

This area has a troubled history, with a lot of war, *famine*, and disease.

Count Dracula had made hotel *reservations* for me.

JONATHAN HARKER?

YES.

The old woman smiled and gave a message to an old man.

He left and then returned with a letter for me.

My friend,

Welcome to my beautiful land. Tomorrow, a **coach** will take you to the Borgo Pass. My carriage will be waiting there to bring you to me.

I hope you will enjoy your stay.

Your friend,
Dracula

I put my fears behind me as we drove through beautiful **scenery.**

Sometimes the hills were so steep that the horses pulling the **coach** were forced to go very slowly.

We finally reached the Borgo Pass.

THE OTHER CARRIAGE IS NOT HERE YET.

HE WILL HAVE TO GO WITH US TO BUKOVINA.

While he was speaking, the horses started to go wild. A carriage approached us.

YOU ARE EARLY TONIGHT.

THE ENGLISHMAN WAS IN A HURRY.

IS THAT WHY YOU WANTED TO TAKE HIM TO BUKOVINA?

YOU CANNOT FOOL ME. I KNOW TOO MUCH, AND MY HORSES ARE QUICK.

Dead people travel fast.

My bags were put into the carriage.

As we drove away, dogs began to howl.

Soon, the air was full of howling, and I could hear wolves in the distance.

AARRRRWHOOOOOOOOOOOOOOOOOoo
AARRRRWHOOOOOOOOOOOOOOOOOOoo

Then I saw a faint blue flame.

The driver went toward the flame.

The moon appeared, and I could see a circle of wolves.

The wolves ran away as the driver lifted his arms.

I was too scared to speak or move.

We continued to drive higher and higher into the mountains.

PLEASE HAVE A SEAT. I WILL NOT JOIN YOU BECAUSE I HAVE ALREADY EATEN.

As I was eating, Count Dracula asked me about my journey. I told him about everything I had seen.

He leaned close to me, and it made me **shudder**. He had really bad breath. Being around him made me feel sick.

He must have noticed, because he moved away from me.

I could see it was getting light outside, and I could hear the wolves.

AH, THE CHILDREN OF THE NIGHT ~ WHAT MUSIC THEY MAKE!

AARRRRWHOOOOOOOOOOOOOOO

YOU MUST BE TIRED. YOUR BEDROOM IS READY. YOU CAN SLEEP AS LONG AS YOU WANT TOMORROW.

IF I WERE IN LONDON, IT WOULD BE OBVIOUS THAT I AM A STRANGER.

YOU WILL STAY HERE WITH ME SO THAT I CAN LEARN TO SPEAK ENGLISH BETTER.

I AM HAPPY TO DO THAT. CAN I VISIT THIS ROOM WHENEVER I WANT?

YOU MAY GO ANYWHERE IN THE CASTLE, EXCEPT WHERE THE DOORS ARE LOCKED. YOU WOULD NOT WANT TO GO IN THOSE ROOMS.

TRANSYLVANIA IS NOT ENGLAND. OUR WAYS ARE NOT YOUR WAYS, AND YOU MIGHT SEE THINGS THAT LOOK STRANGE TO YOU.

LIKE THE BLUE FLAME?

PEOPLE BELIEVE THE BLUE FLAME APPEARS AT THE SITE OF HIDDEN **TREASURE**.

BECAUSE **PEASANTS** ARE FOOLISH. THE FLAME ONLY APPEARS ON ONE NIGHT OF THE YEAR. NO ONE DARES TO GO OUTSIDE ON THAT NIGHT.

YOU WOULD NOT BE ABLE TO FIND THESE PLACES IN THE DAYLIGHT.

THAT IS TRUE.

BUT HOW CAN IT STAY HIDDEN WHEN THE FLAME SHOWS WHERE IT IS?

BUT TELL ME ABOUT LONDON AND ABOUT THE HOUSE THAT YOU AND PETER HAWKINS HAVE FOUND FOR ME.

THE **ESTATE** IS CALLED CARFAX —

IT IS LARGE AND SURROUNDED BY A SOLID STONE WALL.

THERE IS ONLY ONE HOUSE NEARBY. IT IS A PRIVATE *INSANE ASYLUM.*

I AM GLAD IT IS OLD AND BIG.

May 8
I only slept a few hours; then I got up. I was just starting to shave when ...

GOOD MORNING.

I AM NO LONGER YOUNG, AND MY HEART IS HEAVY FROM ALL THESE SAD YEARS **MOURNING** THE DEAD.

I LIKE TO BE ALONE WITH MY THOUGHTS.

His words did not match the expression on his face.

I jumped and cut myself. I hadn't seen Count Dracula come in. He did not have a reflection in the mirror.

HISS!

He reached for my throat. I stepped back and his hand touched the beads of my *crucifix.*

He *immediately* calmed down.

BE CAREFUL. IT IS DANGEROUS TO CUT YOURSELF IN THIS COUNTRY.

THIS MIRROR IS TO BLAME.

AWAY WITH IT!

He threw the mirror out of the window and it shattered below.

How am I going to shave now?

SMASH

I ate breakfast alone. I could not find Count Dracula anywhere, so I explored the castle.

There were doors everywhere, and they were all locked.

THIS CASTLE IS A PRISON, AND I AM A PRISONER!

CHAPTER THREE

Midnight

WE **SZEKELYS** ARE A PROUD **RACE**. IT WAS ONE OF OUR OWN WHO BEAT THE TURKISH ON THEIR OWN LAND.

BUT THE DAYS OF WAR ARE OVER. BLOOD IS TOO **PRECIOUS** IN THESE DAYS OF PEACE.

May 12
He asked me a lot of questions about law, lawyers, and shipping things to England.

COULD I DO THIS MYSELF?

YOU COULD.

GOOD!

THEN WRITE TO PETER HAWKINS AND TELL HIM YOU WILL STAY HERE ANOTHER MONTH.

*I became **depressed** at the thought of staying longer.*

DO YOU REALLY NEED ME TO STAY SO LONG?

I WON'T TAKE NO FOR AN ANSWER. WHEN YOU WRITE TO HIM, MAKE SURE YOU ONLY TALK ABOUT **BUSINESS**.

THE SAME GOES FOR ALL OF YOUR LETTERS.

I AM SURE YOUR FRIENDS WOULD BE PLEASED TO KNOW YOU ARE WELL.

I HAVE TO WARN YOU. IF YOU GO TO ANOTHER PART OF THE CASTLE, MAKE SURE YOU DO NOT FALL ASLEEP THERE.

THIS PLACE IS OLD, AND YOU WILL HAVE BAD DREAMS.

YOU WILL BE SAFE IN YOUR OWN ROOM.

*I have placed the **crucifix** over my bed. I believe it will keep him away from me. I will sleep safely.*

I am safe in my room. Those awful women who want to suck my blood cannot get me in here.

May 19
Count Dracula told me to write three letters: one (June 12) saying that my work here was almost done; another (June 19) that I was heading home the next morning; and the third (June 29) that I had left the castle and arrived at Bistritz.

Now I know how long I have to live. God help me!

May 28
There is a chance of escape ....

SOME TRAVELERS HAVE GIVEN ME THESE LETTERS.

THEY ARE AN INSULT TO MY FRIENDSHIP AND **HOSPITALITY!**

... or at least to send word home. Some travelers have come to the castle. Maybe they can mail some letters home for me.

21

May 31
When I woke up, every piece of paper – all my notes – were gone.

June 17
Two wagons delivered many large, empty boxes to the castle.

June 24
I heard the **miserable** cry of a woman.

I heard Count Dracula's voice. He was answered by the howling of wolves.

GRRRAAAH

MONSTER, GIVE ME MY CHILD!

No more noises came from the woman.

I did not feel bad for her. She was better off dead.

GRRRR

June 25, Morning

I NEED TO DO SOMETHING! IF I CAN JUST GET INTO COUNT DRACULA'S ROOM.

BUT IT IS IMPOSSIBLE – THE DOOR IS ALWAYS LOCKED. BUT IF HE CAN CRAWL FROM HIS WINDOW, SO CAN I.

How can I escape?

I stepped out ...

... and reached Count Dracula's window.

I HAVE TO KEEP GOING.

Except for a large amount of gold, the room was empty.

A heavy door led to a stone passage with a staircase.

I went down the stairs.

I found an old *chapel* that smelled like dirt.

The boxes I saw being delivered were filled with dirt.

I went closer.

There, in one of the large boxes, lay Count Dracula!

I couldn't tell if he was dead or asleep. I hurried back to my own room to think about what I had seen.

June 29
Today is the date of my last letter. I saw Count Dracula leave the castle by the same window, but he was wearing my clothes. I went back to the library and fell asleep.

Count Dracula woke me up.

TOMORROW, MY FRIEND, WE MUST PART. YOU WILL RETURN TO ENGLAND.

YOUR LETTER HOME HAS BEEN SENT. EVERYTHING WILL BE READY FOR YOUR JOURNEY.

CAN I LEAVE TONIGHT?

MY CARRIAGE IS NOT HERE.

I WOULD BE HAPPY TO WALK.

He opened the door.

THEN YOU MAY LEAVE.

HROOOHHH

I would be attacked by wolves.

The thought of me helping this monster live in London made me angry. I had to *destroy* him.

His eyes looked at me, and I froze.

The shovel fell from my hand, making a deep gash in his forehead.

PANK

I couldn't think straight. Hearing heavy wagons nearing the castle, I ran ...

... back into Count Dracula's room. I heard the boxes being nailed shut. They were carried away on the wagons.

CHAPTER FIVE

Letter from Miss Mina Murray
to Miss Lucy Westenra

May 9

My dearest Lucy,

I long to be with you by the sea, where we can talk freely. I have been working very hard lately. I have also been learning **shorthand** so that I may help Jonathan after we are married.

He wrote a short letter to me from Transylvania. He is well and will be returning soon.

Yours,
Mina

P.S. What are the **rumors** I hear about you and a tall, handsome man?

Letter from Miss Lucy Westenra to Miss Mina Murray

May 18

My dearest Mina,

Someone has been telling stories! The man is Arthur Holmwood, and he often visits. He has introduced Mama and me to a very clever man, Dr. Jack Seward. Dr. Seward runs an __insane asylum__. He is one of the most __confident__ men I have ever met.

Mina, I want to share a secret with you.

I love Arthur Holmwood!

I think he loves me, too.

Good night,

Lucy

P.S. Remember, this is a secret between us.

Letter from Miss Lucy Westenra to Miss Mina Murray

May 24

My Dear,

Today I had three men **propose** marriage to me!

The first came just before lunch from Dr. Jack Seward.

LUCY, YOU ARE VERY DEAR TO ME. IF WE WERE TOGETHER ...

He saw me cry ...

... I AM SORRY. I DON'T WANT TO **UPSET** YOU.

DO YOU CARE FOR SOMEONE ELSE?

YES.

THEN I HOPE YOU WILL BE HAPPY WITH HIM. I WILL STILL BE YOUR FRIEND.

It is nice to be **proposed** to, but sad to see a good man leave broken-hearted.

The second **proposal** came after lunch, from an American, Mr. Quincey Morris.

MISS LUCY, I KNOW I AIN'T TOO FANCY, BUT HOW ABOUT WE **HITCH** UP TOGETHER AND RIDE OFF INTO THE SUNSET?

I DO NOT KNOW ANYTHING ABOUT **HITCHING**.

BE HONEST WITH ME – IS THERE ANYONE ELSE YOU CARE FOR?

IF THERE IS, I WON'T TROUBLE YOU ANYMORE, AND I WILL STAY YOUR FAITHFUL FRIEND.

I cried.

Even so, I was able to tell him the truth.

THERE IS SOMEONE I LOVE, THOUGH HE HAS NOT SAID THAT HE LOVES ME.

DON'T CRY.

HE'D BETTER SAY HE LOVES YOU SOON, OR HE'LL HAVE ME TO DEAL WITH.

THANK YOU FOR YOUR HONESTY. GOOD-BYE.

WHY MUST A MAN LIKE THAT BE MADE UNHAPPY WHEN THERE ARE HUNDREDS OF GIRLS WHO WOULD WORSHIP THE VERY GROUND HE STANDS ON?

Do I have to tell you about my third proposal? It was from Arthur Holmwood.

I am very, very happy, and I do not know what I have done to deserve such a husband and such a friend.

Dr. Seward's Diary
(recorded by phonograph)
May 25

Cannot eat or rest since Lucy's rejection of me yesterday. Nothing seems worth doing today.

THE ONLY CURE IS WORK, SO I WENT TO SEE MY PATIENTS.

ONE OF THEM FASCINATES ME.

Renfield - Hopeful, strong and excitable, but sometimes gloomy.

June 5
Renfield has a strange love for animals. Right now he is busy catching flies.

June 18
He has switched to spiders.

He feeds the flies to them and uses his own food to get more flies.

CHAPTER SIX

Mina Murray's Journal
July 24
Whitby

It is lovely to be with Lucy in this beautiful place again.

They have a **legend** here that bells are heard out at sea when a ship is lost. I must ask the old man about this.

August 1

Mr. Swales tells me he is nearly a hundred. He is very **skeptical**.

ALL OF THIS TALK ABOUT GHOSTS AND SUCH IS **NONSENSE**. IT MAKES ME ANGRY TO THINK ABOUT IT.

We stayed a while. Lucy told me all about her wedding plans with Arthur. It made me miss Jonathan even more.

I wish he was here – I haven't heard from him for a whole month.

Dr. Seward's Diary
July 1
Renfield's spiders are annoying. I have told him he must get rid of them.

BUZZIII

He wasn't happy about it.

While I was there, I saw him catch a fly and eat it.

I **scolded** him, but he argued ...

IT IS GOOD FOR ME. IT IS LIFE AND GIVES LIFE TO ME.

I must watch how he gets rid of his spiders.

July 8
There is a reason Renfield behaves so strangely. He has a new pet - a sparrow - and he has already started to **tame** it.

July 19
Renfield now has many sparrows. His flies and spiders are almost all gone.

I NEED TO ASK A *FAVOR*, DOCTOR.

WHAT IS IT?

I WOULD LIKE A KITTEN THAT I CAN PLAY WITH, AND FEED AND FEED!

THAT IS NOT POSSIBLE.

Happiness left his face ...

... and it took on a look of murder.

I will be careful to see how this turns out.

July 20
There were feathers and a few drops of blood in Renfield's room.

WHERE ARE THE BIRDS?

THEY FLEW AWAY.

I THINK HE ATE THEM.

I gave Renfield a drug to make him sleep. He wants to take in as many lives as he can. He gave many flies to one spider, many spiders to one bird, and then wanted a cat to eat many birds.

What will he do next?

How many lives does he think make up a human?

OH LUCY, I CANNOT BE ANGRY WITH YOU. AND I CANNOT BE ANGRY WITH MY FRIEND ARTHUR WHO HAS MADE YOU HAPPY. INSTEAD, I MUST WORK AND WORK.

IF ONLY I HAD SOME REASON TO KEEP GOING!

Mina Murray's Journal
July 26

I am worried about Jonathan. I haven't heard from him, although Mr. Hawkins tells me he is on his way home. It is not like Jonathan to *ignore* me.

Lucy has started to walk in her sleep. Her mother told me to lock the door of our room every night.

She is to be married in autumn to Arthur Holmwood, the only son of **Lord** Godalming. Arthur will be here as soon as he can leave town – his father is not well.

August 6
Still no news.
The weather is growing dark and scary.

Mr. Swales was nervous.

MY TIME IS NEAR. I'M NOT AFRAID OF DYING, BUT THERE IS SOMETHING IN THAT WIND THAT SMELLS LIKE DEATH.

IT'S IN THE AIR. I FEEL IT COMING.

I was upset to hear that. I was glad when a **coast guard** came along. He was looking out at an unusual ship.

IT LOOKS LIKE A RUSSIAN SHIP, BUT IT IS MOVING IN A STRANGE WAY.

THERE'S A STORM COMING, AND IT DOESN'T SEEM TO KNOW HOW TO ESCAPE IT.

CHAPTER SEVEN

NEWSPAPER CLIPPING FROM *THE DAILY GRAPH*, AUGUST 8
Last night saw one of the **fiercest** storms ever to hit the area. The waves **rose**, and the wind forced a strange ship into the **harbor**.

The ship was **deserted**, except for the dead captain who had tied himself to the ship's **wheel**.

Somehow, the ship arrived in the **harbor**.

AUGUST 9
It was a Russian ship called *The Demeter*. It came from Varna and carried many large wooden boxes filled with dirt. A Whitby lawyer, Mr. S. F. Billington, took the boxes.

There was a lot of interest in a large dog which came onshore when the ship landed in the **harbor**.

It later attacked and killed another large dog in the town by tearing out its throat.

The *Demeter* Captain's Log

(Varna to Whitby)

July 6 — Set sail.

July 13 — **Crew** unhappy about something.

July 14 — Worried about **crew**. They seem nervous.

July 16 — Petrofsky is missing.

July 17 — Olgaren says there is a strange man on **board**. We found no one.

July 24 — Ship seems **doomed**. Another man is lost.

July 28 — Four days in a storm.

July 29 — Night watchman lost.

July 30 — Two more lost. Only myself, first mate, and one hand left.

August 1 — Two days of fog.

August 2 — One more gone. God help us!

Mina Murray's Journal
August 10
The funeral for the poor captain was very touching. Lucy seemed very **upset**. Her dreams are having an effect on her.

Poor old Mr. Swales was found dead with a broken neck this morning. He must have fallen backward in fear. There was a look of **horror** on his face. Perhaps he had seen death with his dying eyes.

August 11, 3 a.m. CHAPTER EIGHT
I have just had a horrible adventure.

I woke up and found Lucy's bed empty.

When I couldn't find her in the house ...

... I went outside.

I thought I would look by our favorite spot.

I saw a **pale** figure there with something dark – some man or monster – bent over it.

LUCY!

The dark figure raised its head.

Lucy did not answer.

As I got closer, I saw she was alone.

Lucy was in a deep sleep and **struggling** to breathe.

I took her home. No one saw us.

MINA, PROMISE NOT TO TELL ANYONE ABOUT THIS – NOT EVEN MY MOTHER.

I PROMISE.

I put a shawl around her throat with a safety pin. She moaned.

I must have caught her throat with the safety pin, because the skin was **pierced**.

Letter from Samuel F. Billington and Son, Lawyers, Whitby, to Mr. Carter Paterson and Co., London

August 17

Dear Sirs,

Please deliver the **shipment** to Carfax **immediately**.

The house is empty. The keys are **enclosed**. They are all labeled.

Please leave the fifty boxes in the old **chapel** of the mansion.

Once delivered, you are to leave the keys in the main hall of the house.

Faithfully yours,
Samuel F. Billington and Son

Mina Murray's Journal
August 13
I woke up during the night and found Lucy looking out of the window. But, she was asleep!

THERE ARE HIS RED EYES AGAIN!

August 15
Lucy slept late. Arthur's father is better, and they will get married soon. Lucy's mother is both sad and happy.

I AM SAD TO LOSE LUCY, BUT I AM HAPPY THAT SHE WILL HAVE SOMEONE TO TAKE CARE OF HER. YOU MUST KEEP THIS SECRET, MINA – THE DOCTOR SAYS I DO NOT HAVE LONG TO LIVE. MY HEART IS WEAK AND ANY SUDDEN SHOCK WILL KILL ME.

It was a good decision to not tell her about that awful night when Lucy went sleepwalking.

August 17
No news from Jonathan. Lucy is growing weaker.

THE TINY WOUNDS ON HER THROAT SEEM TO BE GETTING WORSE.

I HAVE TO TAKE HER TO A DOCTOR.

August 19
Lucy is slightly better. She slept well last night.

AT LAST, NEWS OF JONATHAN! HE HAS BEEN SICK. I WILL GO AND TAKE CARE OF HIM. AND I WILL BRING HIM HOME.

43

Letter from Sister Agatha, Hospital of St. Joseph and Saint Mary, Buda-Pesth, to Miss Mina Murray

Dear Madam,

Mr. Jonathan Harker has asked me to write to you. He has been here for six weeks. He is suffering from a violent brain fever.

He sends his love and will return to you as soon as he is well enough to travel.

He has talked about many strange and scary things while in this troubled state. But do not worry, he is being cared for here. He will soon be well enough to go home.

Sister Agatha

Dr. Seward's Diary
August 19
Sudden change in Renfield last night. He would not talk with the **attendant**.

WHERE ARE YOUR PETS?

I DON'T CARE ABOUT THEM NOW.

THE MASTER IS COMING.

DON'T YOU CARE ABOUT YOUR SPIDERS?

THE BRIDESMAIDS MAY LOOK PRETTY TO THE CROWD, BUT WHEN THE BRIDE APPEARS, EVERYONE LOOKS AT HER.

After midnight, the night watchman told me that Renfield had escaped.

He would not explain himself.

I ran outside **immediately**.

I saw someone climbing the high wall between our grounds and Carfax, the **deserted** house next door.

GET SOME MEN AND FOLLOW ME TO CARFAX.

Renfield was pressed against the oak door of the **chapel**.

I AM HERE TO DO AS YOU WISH, MASTER. I AM YOUR SERVANT AND YOU WILL REWARD ME.

I HAVE *WORSHIPPED* YOU *FAITHFULLY*, AND I AM WAITING FOR YOUR INSTRUCTIONS.

He was more like a wild beast than a man.

ALGGHGH

I WILL BE PATIENT, MASTER. IT IS COMING!

He is safe now. His cries are awful, but it is worse when he is quiet.

CHAPTER NINE

Letter from Miss Mina Harker to Miss Lucy Westenra
Budapest
August 24
My dearest Lucy,

I am with Jonathan. He is so thin and **pale**, and he doesn't remember anything that happened.

He has suffered some terrible shock.

MINA, MY DEAR, YOU KNOW THAT THERE SHOULD BE NO SECRETS BETWEEN A MAN AND WIFE.

I MIGHT HAVE IMAGINED EVERYTHING. IT IS ALL WRITTEN IN THIS NOTEBOOK.

PLEASE KEEP IT. READ IT IF YOU WANT, BUT DO NOT REMIND ME OF WHAT I WENT THROUGH.

He was **exhausted**. I asked Sister Agatha to let us get married as soon as possible.

THAT AFTERNOON ...

I WILL.

I AM THE HAPPIEST WOMAN ALIVE.

I WILL LOVE YOU FOR THE REST OF MY LIFE.

We *sealed* our wedding vows with a kiss ...

Letter from Miss Lucy Westenra to Miss Mina Harker

Whitby,
August 30

My dearest Mina,

I send all my love to you and your husband. I hope you will return to England soon. I am feeling much better. Arthur is with me, and we are getting married on September 28.

Lucy

Dr. Seward's Diary

August 23

Renfield escaped to Carfax again last night.

ARGH!

He went crazy when he saw me. I am sure he would have killed me, but ...

... suddenly, he was calm. I saw him looking at a large bat flying off to the west.

I WILL GO QUIETLY.

We returned to the house without any trouble.

Lucy Westenra's Diary

August 25

More bad dreams. I wish I could remember them. This morning I am **pale** and weak. My throat hurts and I am having trouble breathing.

Letter from Arthur Holmwood to Dr. Seward

August 31

My dear Jack,

I want you to do me a **favor**. Lucy is sick and she is getting worse every day. Although it will be painful for you, I need to ask you to see her.

Do not fail!

ARTHUR

Letter from Dr. Seward to Arthur Holmwood

Miss Westenra seems to be generally well. She sweetly said:

I DO NOT LIKE TALKING ABOUT MYSELF.

I WILL NOT REPEAT ANYTHING YOU SAY, BUT ARTHUR IS WORRIED ABOUT YOU.

YOU CAN TELL ARTHUR EVERYTHING.

It seems like her **blood levels** are low.

She happened to cut herself by accident and I got a small sample of blood to **analyze**.

Everything looks normal – her sickness must be of the mind.

Letter From Dr. Seward to
Arthur Holmwood
(continued)

I wrote to my old friend,
Professor Van Helsing, of
Amsterdam. He is an expert on
strange diseases.

He is a very smart and **noble**
man. I asked him to come here
quickly.

Yours always,
Jack Seward

Letter from Abraham Van Helsing
to Dr. Seward

September 2

My Good Friend,

I am coming to you immediately.

49

Let me see the young lady right away. I might have to return home that same night.

If I am needed, I will come again three days later and stay as long as you like.

Van Helsing

PROFESSOR!

ARTHUR HOLMWOOD HAS PLACED ALL HIS TRUST IN ME.

YOU MUST TELL ARTHUR WHAT YOU THINK. THIS IS A MATTER OF LIFE AND DEATH – MAYBE MORE.

I asked him what he meant ...

... but he would not tell me.

HILLINGHAM, NEAR LONDON

IT IS A PLEASURE TO MEET YOU, MISS. THOSE WHO LOVE YOU TOLD ME YOU WERE SICK. TO THEM I SAY "POUF!"

WE WILL PROVE THEM WRONG.

click

WHY DON'T WE SEND DR. SEWARD AWAY WHILE YOU TELL ME ALL ABOUT YOUR TROUBLES?

A LITTLE LATER ...

JACK!

I MUST GO BACK HOME TO THINK. SEND ME A TELEGRAM EVERY DAY. I WILL RETURN WHEN YOU NEED ME TO.

THIS SICKNESS INTRIGUES ME.

51

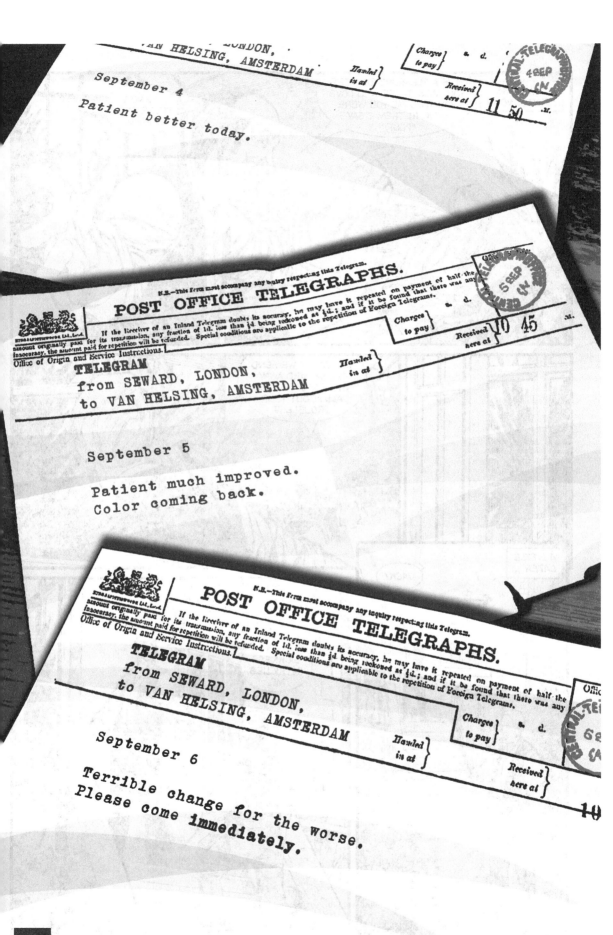

VAN HELSING, AMSTERDAM

September 4

Patient better today.

POST OFFICE TELEGRAPHS.

TELEGRAM
from SEWARD, LONDON,
to VAN HELSING, AMSTERDAM

September 5

Patient much improved.
Color coming back.

POST OFFICE TELEGRAPHS.

TELEGRAM
from SEWARD, LONDON,
to VAN HELSING, AMSTERDAM

September 6

Terrible change for the worse.
Please come immediately.

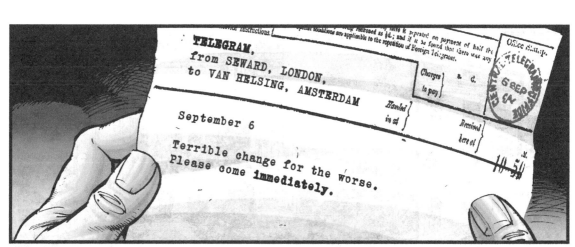

TELEGRAM,
from SEWARD, LONDON,
to VAN HELSING, AMSTERDAM

September 6

Terrible change for the worse.
Please come **immediately**.

CHAPTER TEN

LIVERPOOL STREET
STATION, LONDON
SEPTEMBER 7

HAVE YOU SAID ANYTHING TO ARTHUR, HER FIANCÉ?

NO, I WAITED UNTIL I HAD SEEN YOU.

IT IS BETTER THAT HE DOES NOT KNOW YET.

I HAVE A FEW THOUGHTS WHICH I WILL SHARE WITH YOU LATER.

WHY NOT NOW? I MIGHT BE ABLE TO HELP YOU.

REMEMBER THAT KNOWLEDGE IS STRONGER THAN MEMORY. YOU MUST **RECORD** EVERYTHING.

WE LEARN FROM FAILURE, NOT FROM SUCCESS!

HILLINGHAM,
NEAR LONDON

Dr. Seward's Diary
September 7
Lucy's mother was worried. I told her to try not to think about her daughter's sickness. She led us up to Lucy's room.

Lucy was very sick and **struggling** to breathe.

OH MY! THIS IS TERRIBLE.

THERE IS NO TIME TO LOSE. WE HAVE TO GIVE HER MORE BLOOD.

I CAN GIVE HER MY BLOOD.

THEN PLEASE GET READY RIGHT NOW.

ARTHUR!

I WAS SO WORRIED, JACK. I HAD TO COME.

YOU ARE JUST IN TIME. SHE NEEDS BLOOD URGENTLY.

54

I WOULD GIVE EVERY DROP OF BLOOD I HAVE FOR HER.

I DO NOT NEED QUITE THAT MUCH!

I WOULD GLADLY DIE TO SAVE HER.

YOU ARE A GOOD MAN TO HELP THE ONE YOU LOVE.

After the transfusion ...

PLEASE WATCH OUR BRAVE YOUNG MAN. HE MUST REST, EAT, AND SLEEP.

ARTHUR, YOU SAVED HER LIFE.

When Arthur left ...

WHAT DO YOU THINK ABOUT THAT MARK ON HER THROAT?

I DON'T KNOW WHAT IT COULD BE.

I HAVE TO GO BACK TO AMSTERDAM TONIGHT TO RESEARCH IT.

STAY HERE AND WATCH HER ALL NIGHT.

I wondered if the mark would explain how she lost so much blood.

September 8
I sat up all night with Lucy. She slept well.

I went home. Van Helsing sent me a **telegram** telling me to return to Lucy that night and meet him there in the morning.

September 9
I was very tired when I got to Hillingham. I hadn't slept for two days.

I AM FEELING BETTER NOW. THERE IS NO NEED FOR YOU TO WATCH ME TONIGHT. YOU HAVE TO SLEEP.

I did not argue with her.

After supper, Lucy brought me to a room next to hers.

YOU CAN SLEEP HERE. I WILL LEAVE THE DOORS OPEN. IF I WANT ANYTHING, I WILL CALL FOR YOU.

I lay on the sofa and went to sleep.

September 10
Van Helsing arrived.

HOW IS OUR PATIENT?

SHE WAS WELL WHEN I LAST SAW HER.

LET'S GO TAKE A LOOK.

OH, NO!

QUICK! HER HEART IS STILL BEATING. EVERYTHING WE DID IS USELESS NOW. WE HAVE TO BEGIN AGAIN.

We started the blood **transfusion** right away.

STAY STILL. WE HAVE TO KEEP HER ASLEEP WHILE HER STRENGTH RETURNS.

Lucy began to look better.

YOU TOOK A LOT MORE BLOOD FROM ARTHUR.

HE IS HER **FIANCÉ.** YOU HAVE WORK TO DO. THIS IS ENOUGH BLOOD FOR NOW. WE SHOULD NOT TELL ARTHUR ABOUT THIS. HE MIGHT BE JEALOUS.

GO HOME AND GET STRONG AGAIN. I WILL WATCH OVER HER.

GOOD NIGHT.

GOOD NIGHT.

September 11
I went to Hillingham.
Lucy was much better.
She did not seem to
remember anything
that had happened.

WE OWE YOU SO MUCH, DR. SEWARD, BUT YOU SHOULD TAKE CARE OF YOURSELF NOW.

YOU LOOK PALE.

A package arrived for Van Helsing.

THIS IS FOR YOU, MISS LUCY.

FOR ME?

YES, BUT IT'S NOT TO PLAY WITH. IT IS MEDICINE.

I PUT SOME ON YOUR WINDOW AND AROUND YOUR NECK. NOW YOU'LL BE ABLE TO SLEEP WELL.

IS THIS A JOKE? THIS IS GARLIC!

FLING

I NEVER JOKE. THIS IS FOR YOUR OWN GOOD.

SOMEONE MIGHT THINK YOU ARE USING A SPELL TO KEEP AN EVIL SPIRIT OUT.

PERHAPS I AM!

CHAPTER ELEVEN

September 13
Van Helsing and I arrived at Hillingham early in the morning.

We met with Lucy's mother.

LUCY SEEMS BETTER. SHE IS STILL ASLEEP.

AHA! MY **TREATMENT** IS WORKING.

YOU CANNOT **TAKE ALL THE CREDIT.**

SHE IS SLEEPING MUCH BETTER SINCE I GOT RID OF THOSE HORRIBLE SMELLING FLOWERS AND OPENED HER WINDOW TO LET SOME FRESH AIR IN.

NO!

LUCY'S MOTHER HAS DONE SOMETHING VERY HARMFUL! WE MUST NOT TELL HER OR THE SHOCK MIGHT KILL HER.

ALL THE POWER OF EVIL SEEMS TO BE WORKING AGAINST US.

AS I EXPECTED. I MUST GIVE BLOOD THIS TIME.

The **transfusion** worked once more, and Lucy felt better again. Van Helsing said he would watch over her for the next two nights.

59

Lucy Westenra's Diary
September 17
Four days and nights of peace. No flapping noise at the window and no quiet voices **commanding** me to do strange things.

I am not afraid to sleep now. And I am starting to like the smell of **garlic**.

Van Helsing doesn't need to watch over me now. I woke up twice last night to see him asleep in his chair. I went back to sleep even though I heard something by my window.

Newspaper Clipping from *The Pall Mall Gazette*, September 18
THE ESCAPED WOLF
Interview with the zoo keeper.

BERSICKER!

RRNARRRH

He never gave us any trouble before. It just goes to show – you can't trust wolves.

He lifted his hat and walked off, as polite as a **lord**. Bersicker rested all evening.

AS SOON AS THE MOON CAME OUT, THE WOLVES STARTED HOWLING.

WHEN I CHECKED ON BERSICKER'S CAGE JUST BEFORE MIDNIGHT, THE BARS WERE TWISTED AND BERSICKER WAS GONE.

September 18

THE ESCAPED WOLF

Interview with the Keeper in the Zoological Gardens.

DID ANYONE SEE ANYTHING? CAN YOU EXPLAIN HOW THE WOLF ESCAPED?

ONE OF OUR GARDENERS SAW A BIG GRAY DOG, BUT I DON'T THINK IT MADE ANY DIFFERENCE.

I THINK BERSICKER JUST WANTED TO GET OUT.

HOW STRANGE! BERSICKER IS BACK!

The wicked wolf that had terrified London had returned to his cage, as **tame** as a lamb.

HE'S GOTTEN INTO SOME SORT OF TROUBLE. HE HAS GLASS CUTS ON HIM.

Dr. Seward's Diary
September 17
I was in my **study** updating my **records**.

Suddenly, Renfield rushed in and started to attack me.

YAH!

He caught me by surprise and hurt me.

I was forced to hit him.

THWAK

When the **attendants** rushed in, Renfield was on the floor. He was licking up my blood like a dog.

BLOOD IS LIFE!

Note written by Lucy Westenra
September 17, night

I am writing this for someone to find. I am weak and dying, but I must write this down.

I went to bed with the **garlic** in its usual place. I fell asleep quickly.

A bat flapped by my window and woke me. I was scared.

flap flap flap

IS ANYBODY THERE?

There was no answer, and I did not want to wake my mother up.

I went to the window ...

flap flap flap

HOOOOWWW

... but I could not see anything except a large bat, so I went back to bed.

Mother came in.

I WAS WORRIED ABOUT YOU – ARE YOU ALL RIGHT?

YOU WILL CATCH A COLD SITTING THERE. COME AND SLEEP WITH ME.

The flapping and howling continued.

HOOOOWWW

flap flap flap

WHAT IS THAT?

AAIEEE!

SKVVVASH

RRRRRRRr

A horrible noise came from mother ...

GGGUUUGH!

Something like dust came blowing in through the window. I was frozen, as if in some kind of *trance.*

CHAPTER TWELVE

Dr. Seward's Diary
September 18
I went to Hillingham with
Van Helsing. No one answered
the door. Every window and
door was locked.

We knew something
was wrong and
decided to break in.

QUICK!

IT IS NOT
TOO LATE! GO
WAKE THE MAIDS UP!
HAVE THEM PREPARE
A WARM BATH.

WE WILL NEED
TO WARM LUCY UP
BEFORE WE CAN DO
ANYTHING ELSE.

THIS IS A
FIGHT TO THE
DEATH.

IF THAT WAS ALL IT
WAS, WE COULD STOP
RIGHT NOW.

LUCY
NEEDS MORE
BLOOD, BUT WE
DO NOT HAVE ANY
MORE. WHAT ARE
WE GOING
TO DO?

IS THERE ANYTHING
WRONG WITH MY
BLOOD?

QUINCEY
MORRIS!

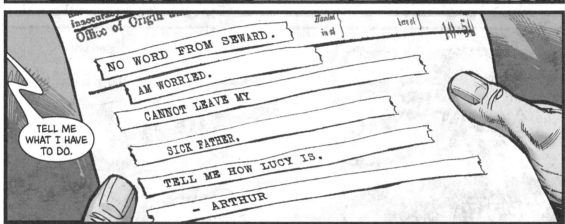

NO WORD FROM SEWARD.

AM WORRIED.

CANNOT LEAVE MY

SICK FATHER,

TELL ME HOW LUCY IS.

— ARTHUR

Lucy **struggled** back to life. Van Helsing handed me a note that had fallen out of her clothing.

Lucy woke up in the afternoon. She realized that her mother was dead. We tried our best to comfort her.

September 19
Lucy slept badly. Van Helsing and I watched over her, while Quincey guarded the house.

She saw Arthur in the afternoon. Seeing him made her a little happier.

Letter from Mrs. Mina Harker to Miss Lucy Westenra (unopened)

September 17

My dearest Lucy,

We arrived back at Exeter and were greeted by Mr. Hawkins, even though he was sick. We are staying at his house.

From my bedroom, I can see the cathedral. Jonathan and Mr. Hawkins are now **business** partners. They are busy every day.

Letter from Mrs. Mina Harker to Miss Lucy Westenra (unopened)

September 18

My dearest Lucy,

Such sadness. Mr. Hawkins has died suddenly. It is like we have lost a father. Jonathan is **grieving** for the man who was his friend for so long. Mr. Hawkins left Jonathan a **fortune**.

He wished to be buried next to his father in London. Jonathan is in charge of the **funeral arrangements**.

I will try to see you while we are there.

Good-bye, my dearest Lucy. I send you my blessings.

Your loving friend,

Mina Harker

Their eyes met - and the couple parted.

Lucy's eyes closed and she stopped breathing.

Van Helsing placed a small golden **crucifix** over her mouth.

IT IS ALL OVER. SHE IS DEAD!

AT LAST SHE IS AT PEACE. IT IS THE END.

NOT SO - IT IS JUST THE BEGINNING!

BUT WE CANNOT DO ANYTHING YET. WE HAVE TO WAIT AND SEE.

CHAPTER THIRTEEN

We arranged a joint funeral for Lucy and her mother.

TOMORROW I WANT YOU TO BRING ME A SET OF SURGICAL KNIVES.

WE HAVE TO DO AN AUTOPSY?

YES AND NO. I WANT TO CUT OFF HER HEAD AND TAKE OUT HER HEART.

DO NOT BE SHOCKED. TRUST ME – I HAVE A GOOD REASON.

I TRUST YOU.

Later, Van Helsing came into my room.

DO NOT BRING THE KNIVES. WE WILL NOT DO IT.

WHY NOT?

IT IS TOO LATE. THIS CRUCIFIX WAS STOLEN IN THE NIGHT.

BUT YOU HAVE IT NOW.

BECAUSE I GOT IT BACK FROM THE WOMAN WHO STOLE IT FROM LUCY.

SHE WILL BE PUNISHED FOR STEALING FROM THE DEAD.

NOW WE HAVE TO WAIT.

THIS IS GOING TO BE PAINFUL.

That night, Lucy lay in her coffin covered in **garlic** flowers. I slept, but Van Helsing did not go to bed at all.

THE WESTMINSTER GAZETTE

September 25

A HAMPSTEAD MYSTERY

There have been a number of **cases** of very young children returning late from playing on Hampstead Heath.

Some haven't returned until the next morning. They say that they have been with a "beautiful lady."

EEKLY

Price One Penny.

THE WESTMINSTER GAZETTE

The ones who were missing at night have slight **wounds** to the throat, made by some rat or dog.

Police have been instructed to keep a lookout for children and for any stray dog.

CHAPTER FOURTEEN

Mina Harker's Journal
September 23
Jonathan is better after a bad night. I will read the journal he kept when he was at Count Dracula's castle.

POOR THING! HE HAS SUFFERED SO MUCH!

Letter from Van Helsing to Mrs. Mina Harker
September 24
Dear Madam,
I read Miss Lucy Westenra's letters. They show that you were her friend. I need your help.

May I meet with you? You can trust me.
Van Helsing

September 25

DR. VAN HELSING IS HERE.

MADAM MINA, I AM HERE TO DISCUSS MISS LUCY.

I AM HAPPY TO HELP IN ANY WAY I CAN.

CAN YOU PLEASE TELL ME WHAT YOU REMEMBER OF LUCY'S SLEEPWALKING IN WHITBY?

I WROTE IT ALL DOWN.

PLEASE, READ IT WHILE I ORDER LUNCH.

MADAM MINA, THIS INFORMATION IS VERY USEFUL TO ME. YOU AND YOUR HUSBAND ARE VERY NOBLE.

HOW IS MR. HARKER?

HE WAS GETTING BETTER, BUT HE GOT SICK AGAIN WHEN HE SAW SOMEONE IN LONDON HE THOUGHT HE KNEW.

I went with Van Helsing to the train station. He spotted something in a newspaper.

MY GOD! SO SOON!

Dr. Seward's Diary
September 26
Van Helsing came back today. He had last night's newspaper.

A HAMPSTEAD MYSTERY

There have been a number of **cases** of very young children returning late from playing on Hampstead Heath.

Some haven't returned until the next morning. They say that t... have been with a... "beautiful lady."

The one... were mi... night ha... **wounds**... roat, ma... me rat o...

WHAT DO YOU THINK ABOUT THAT?

THE THROAT WOUNDS ARE LIKE LUCY'S.

WHATEVER INJURED HER HAS INJURED THESE CHILDREN AS WELL.

IN SOME PLACES, BATS ARE KNOWN TO ATTACK SAILORS SLEEPING ON DECK AT NIGHT.

IN THE MORNING, THOSE MEN ARE DEAD.

ARE YOU SAYING THAT LUCY WAS BITTEN BY A BAT HERE IN LONDON?

YOU THINK THAT THE BAT THAT MADE THOSE HOLES IN MISS LUCY'S THROAT **WOUNDED** THESE CHILDREN?

YES.

THEN YOU ARE WRONG. IT IS MUCH WORSE.

IT WAS MISS LUCY!

ARE YOU CRAZY?

CHAPTER FIFTEEN

LET'S GO AND SEE ONE OF THE CHILDREN IN THE HOSPITAL. THEN YOU AND I WILL SPEND THE NIGHT IN THE GRAVEYARD WHERE LUCY'S BODY IS.

THIS IS THE KEY TO HER TOMB.

My heart sank. I had the feeling that a terrible night was ahead of us.

The child's throat **wounds** were **identical** to Lucy's.

When it was dark, we climbed over the wall of the graveyard and found Lucy's **tomb**.

81

WHAT IS YOUR PLAN?

I WILL OPEN THE COFFIN TO PROVE THAT I AM RIGHT.

crack

IT'S EMPTY!

DO YOU BELIEVE ME NOW?

HER BODY IS GONE, BUT THAT DOES NOT PROVE ANYTHING.

THAT IS GOOD LOGIC! WE NEED MORE PROOF. WE WILL SPLIT UP AND KEEP WATCH OVER THE GRAVEYARD.

Just after two o'clock I thought I saw a strange figure.

Then I heard someone. It was Van Helsing holding a small child.

NOW DO YOU BELIEVE ME?

NO! IS THE CHILD HURT?

WE WERE JUST IN TIME.

The child's throat did not have any wounds.

Note left by Van Helsing to Jack Seward, M.D.

Tonight I will go to the graveyard alone.

I will make sure Lucy cannot leave her **tomb** by placing a **crucifix** and **garlic** around the door.

She may still be able to get out if she is desperate.

I am not afraid of Miss Lucy. But the one that made Lucy un-dead might visit her **tomb**.

Count Dracula is clever and strong. He gained strength from the blood we all gave to Miss Lucy.

But, he might not visit the **tomb**. He has better places to hunt than a graveyard where there is just one un-dead woman ...

... and one old man.

Dr. Seward's Diary
September 28

MISS LUCY IS DEAD — BUT IF SHE IS NOT?

YOU MEAN SHE WAS BURIED ALIVE?

SHE IS NOT ALIVE, BUT SHE MIGHT BE UN-DEAD.

I NEED YOUR PERMISSION TO DO WHAT I THINK IS RIGHT. MAY I CUT OFF HER HEAD?

NO, YOU MAY NOT!

YOU WILL NOT DO ANYTHING TO HER POOR DEAD BODY.

I HAVE A **DUTY** TO OTHERS, TO YOU, AND TO THE DEAD. I HAVE TO DO IT.

ALL I ASK IS THAT YOU COME WITH ME.

I HAVE TO DO MY **DUTY**, EVEN IF IT KILLS ME.

I WILL GO WITH YOU.

CHAPTER SIXTEEN

We arrived at the graveyard just before midnight.

Lucy's coffin was empty. Van Helsing secured the door with a **holy wafer** ...

SO THAT THE UN-DEAD MAY NOT ENTER.

Clearly, Van Helsing knew what he was doing.

After a long silence ...

Hush!

We saw a white figure carrying something.

My heart grew cold when I saw that it was Lucy Westenra.

=GASP!=

We were horrified.

With an evil look, she threw down the child.

WAHAAAH! AH! AHAH! WAAAAHH!

THUD

She went to Arthur ...

COME TO ME, ARTHUR. LEAVE THESE OTHER PEOPLE.

I HUNGER FOR YOU. WE CAN REST TOGETHER.

Her voice sounded strangely magical.

Arthur seemed like he was in a **trance** ...

... then Van Helsing stepped in.

HISSSSS!

Lucy looked like she wanted to kill him.

HISSSS!

TELL ME, MY FRIEND, MAY I DO MY WORK?

YES! PUT AN END TO THIS!

87

We were terrified. We watched as her body passed through the narrow crack of the closed door to her **tomb**.

COME, MY FRIENDS — WE CANNOT DO ANYTHING ELSE UNTIL TOMORROW.

THIS CHILD WILL BE ALL RIGHT IN THE MORNING.

September 29, night
We went to the **tomb**.

IS THIS REALLY LUCY? OR A DEMON IN HER SHAPE?

IT IS HER — YOU WILL SEE.

THE UN-DEAD CANNOT DIE. THEY HAVE TO KEEP WORKING, MAKING MORE EVIL IN THE WORLD —

— BECAUSE THEIR VICTIMS ALSO BECOME UN-DEAD.

LUCY HAS POWER OVER THE CHILDREN SHE ATTACKED. SHE CAN MAKE THEM COME TO HER.

BUT IF SHE TRULY DIES THEN THEY WILL RETURN TO NORMAL.

THEY WILL BE UNAWARE AND UNCHANGED BY ANYTHING THAT HAS HAPPENED.

AND, WHEN THE UN-DEAD ARE PUT TO REST AS TRUE DEAD, THEIR SOULS ARE SET FREE.

Van Helsing began the prayer ...

... then Arthur hammered the stake.

YOU MAY KISS HER NOW. SHE IS NO LONGER THE UN-DEAD.

SHE IS TRULY DEAD, AND HER SOUL IS SAFE.

Arthur kissed her.

Then Van Helsing did the rest. We removed her head and filled her mouth with **garlic**.

It seemed brighter than usual outside, as if nature was at peace.

ONE TASK IS DONE, BUT A GREATER ONE LIES AHEAD. WE HAVE TO FIND AND KILL THE SOURCE OF ALL THIS SUFFERING.

IT WILL BE DANGEROUS, BUT IT IS OUR DUTY.

DO WE PROMISE TO GO ON TO THE BITTER END?

WE DO.

WE PROMISE.

WE WILL MEET AGAIN IN TWO DAYS. I WILL BRING TWO OTHERS TO HELP US.

Dr. Seward's Diary
September 29
Van Helsing told me to meet Mina Harker at Paddington Station. He showed me copies of the journals she gave to him.

DR. SEWARD?

MRS. HARKER!

I RECOGNIZED YOU FROM DEAR LUCY'S DESCRIPTION.

CHAPTER SEVENTEEN

She blushed.

September 29, Carfax

I had a room ready for Mrs. Harker. I could tell she was a little nervous about being here, knowing that it was an **insane asylum**.

SHE SAYS THAT SHE HAS A LOT TO TELL ME, SO I AM FINISHING MY JOURNAL WHILE I WAIT FOR HER.

I AM SORRY. I THOUGHT YOU WERE TALKING TO SOMEBODY.

NO, I WAS **RECORDING** MY VOICE FOR MY JOURNAL.

THIS IS QUICKER THAN WRITING IN **SHORTHAND!**

I KNOW YOU WERE THERE WHEN LUCY DIED. WILL YOU TELL ME ABOUT IT, PLEASE?

I CANNOT LET YOU HEAR THAT TERRIBLE STORY.

BESIDES, I DO NOT KNOW HOW TO GET TO **SPECIFIC** PARTS OF MY JOURNAL.

THEN LET ME TYPE OUT WHAT YOU SAY IN YOUR JOURNAL ON MY **TYPEWRITER.** YOU CAN TRUST ME.

I TRUST YOU. YOU MAY TAKE THE RECORDINGS.

September 30
Mr. Harker arrived.

I went to see Renfield. His outbreaks always happened when Count Dracula was nearby. Today he was calm. What does it mean?

Mr. Harker brought letters that had to do with the delivery of boxes from Whitby to Carfax. Even though Renfield gave us many clues, it never occurred to me that it could be Count Dracula's hiding place.

DID YOU **TRACK** COUNT DRACULA'S BOXES?

YES. ALL THE BOXES WERE DELIVERED TO THE OLD **CHAPEL** AT CARFAX.

THERE SHOULD BE A TOTAL OF FIFTY BOXES THERE, UNLESS SOME HAVE BEEN REMOVED.

Mina Harker's Journal
September 30
I met with Arthur Holmwood and Quincey Morris today. It was so sad to meet with them. They reminded me of all the hopes Lucy had just a few months ago.

LUCY AND I WERE LIKE SISTERS.

I KNOW THAT YOU LOVED HER, SO LET ME BE LIKE A SISTER TO YOU DURING YOUR SADNESS.

I HAVE SUFFERED SO MUCH. YOUR SYMPATHY MEANS A LOT TO ME.

LET ME BE LIKE A BROTHER TO YOU.

FOR DEAR LUCY'S SAKE.

Dr. Seward's Diary
September 30
Mrs. Harker asked to see Renfield.

RENFIELD, A LADY WOULD LIKE TO SEE YOU. SHE IS VISITING EVERYONE HERE.

LET ME CLEAN UP FIRST.

CHAPTER EIGHTEEN

Renfield swallowed all the flies and spiders he was keeping.

GOOD EVENING, MR. RENFIELD.

I KNOW YOU ARE NOT THE GIRL THE DOCTOR WANTED TO MARRY. SHE IS DEAD.

I USED TO THINK I WOULD LIVE FOREVER IF I KEPT EATING THINGS THAT WERE ALIVE.

chomp crunch gulp

BLOOD IS LIFE – ISN'T THAT TRUE, DOCTOR?

I NEED TO GO AND MEET VAN HELSING AT THE TRAIN STATION.

GOOD-BYE. I HOPE I WILL GET TO SEE YOU AGAIN.

I PRAY TO GOD THAT NEVER HAPPENS. BLESSINGS TO YOU!

NOW WE HAVE TO PLAN OUR ATTACK. WE KNOW THAT FIFTY BOXES OF DIRT WERE DELIVERED AT CARFAX.

SOME OF THESE BOXES HAVE BEEN REMOVED. WE MUST TRACK EACH OF THESE BOXES.

WE MUST EITHER KILL THIS MONSTER IN HIS HOME, OR WE MUST MAKE SURE HE CANNOT SAFELY SLEEP IN THE DIRT.

REMEMBER, HE IS WEAKEST BETWEEN NOON AND SUNSET WHEN HE IS IN THE SHAPE OF A MAN.

MADAM MINA, YOU ARE TOO PRECIOUS. WE CANNOT RISK YOU GETTING HURT.

WE WILL BE MORE WILLING TO ATTACK COUNT DRACULA IF WE KNOW YOU ARE NOT IN ANY DANGER.

WE CANNOT WASTE ANY TIME.

WE SHOULD LOOK IN THE HOUSE RIGHT AWAY.

October 1
Just as we were about to leave ...

RENFIELD WANTS TO SEE YOU RIGHT NOW, DR. SEWARD.

I'LL GO NOW.

MAY I COME ALSO?

ME, TOO?

Jonathan Harker's Journal
October 1, 5 a.m.

Although Renfield *upset* Mina, she looked well. So I felt fine about going with the others to Carfax.

CHAPTER NINETEEN

MY FRIENDS, WE ARE GOING INTO TERRIBLE DANGER.

OUR **ENEMY** HAS THE STRENGTH OF TWENTY MEN. WE CAN PROTECT OURSELVES BY KEEPING THIS NEAR OUR HEARTS.

He held out a small *crucifix*.

It felt like there was someone else there with us.

YOU HAVE STUDIED MAPS OF THIS PLACE, JONATHAN. WHICH WAY TO THE CHAPEL?

I THINK I KNOW. IT WAS LOCKED LAST TIME I WAS HERE.

I led the way.

THIS IS THE SPOT.

The air smelled very bad.

UGH! I CAN SMELL THE MONSTER'S BREATH.

Arthur sprang into action. He swung the door open and whistled loudly.

Dogs answered the whistle.

They rushed to the scene.

The rats ran away or were killed by the dogs.

When they were gone, it felt like an evil spirit had left us.

We did not find anything else in the house.

COUNT DRACULA MUST HAVE GONE SOMEWHERE ELSE.

LET'S GO HOME.

We all slept late, even Mina. It was very difficult to wake her up. She looks *pale* today.

CHAPTER TWENTY

Jonathan Harker's Journal
October 1

I FOUND A WORKMAN WHO KNEW ALL ABOUT COUNT DRACULA'S BOXES.

HE TOOK SIX TO NEW TOWN, SIX TO BERMONDSEY, AND NINE TO AN OLD HOUSE IN PICCADILLY.

HOW DID THE WORKMAN GET INTO THE HOUSE?

A MAN WAS THERE – HE WAS VERY STRONG AND HELPED HIM UNLOAD THE BOXES.

THE WORKMAN TOLD ME WHERE THE HOUSE IS.

GOOD WORK, JONATHAN.

IF WE FIND THE BOXES IN THAT HOUSE, OUR WORK WILL ALMOST BE FINISHED.

HOW ARE WE GOING TO GET INTO THE HOUSE?

WE GOT INTO CARFAX.

BUT THIS HOUSE IS DIFFERENT. IT IS ON A BUSY STREET. SOMEBODY WILL SEE US.

We decided to wait until morning.

Mina's breathing sounds strange. She is pale.

I hope she will be better tomorrow when she returns to Exeter.

CHAPTER TWENTY-ONE

WE NEED TO OPERATE ON HIM. I WILL GET READY.

Renfield seemed **paralyzed.**

GRROANNN ...

Van Helsing quickly returned.

HIS SKULL IS **FRACTURED.** HE CANNOT MOVE BECAUSE OF IT.

WE MUST REDUCE THE PRESSURE IN HIS SKULL.

THERE IS NO TIME TO LOSE. RENFIELD MAY BE ABLE TO TELL US SOMETHING THAT WILL SAVE MANY LIVES.

WE WILL **OPERATE** JUST ABOVE HIS EAR.

Van Helsing performed the **operation.**

Suddenly, Renfield opened his eyes.

Renfield was getting worse by the minute.

DOCTOR, I AM DYING! I ONLY HAVE A FEW MINUTES LEFT.

I HAVE TO TELL YOU SOMETHING.

I WAITED ALL DAY, BUT HE DID NOT SEND ME WHAT HE HAD PROMISED.

AT NIGHT, HE CAME IN THROUGH THE WINDOW AND PASSED BY ME LIKE I WAS NO ONE.

"HE SMELLED DIFFERENT. IT WAS AS IF MRS. HARKER HAD COME INTO THE ROOM."

WHEN MRS. HARKER CAME TO SEE ME THIS AFTERNOON SHE WASN'T THE SAME.

SHE SEEMED *PALE*, LIKE SHE DID NOT HAVE ANY BLOOD.

"I FIGURED OUT THAT COUNT DRACULA HAD BEEN TAKING THE LIFE OUT OF HER."

"IT MADE ME ANGRY. TONIGHT I WAS READY FOR HIM."

"I GRABBED HIM AND THOUGHT I WAS GOING TO WIN — UNTIL I SAW HIS EYES."

HISSSS!

Count Dracula threw his victim down and jumped at us.

But we protected ourselves with **crucifixes**.

HISSSS!

BLAM BLAM

A black cloud floated across the sky, and the **mist** went away.

Mrs. Harker woke from her **trance**.

NEEEAAAARRGH

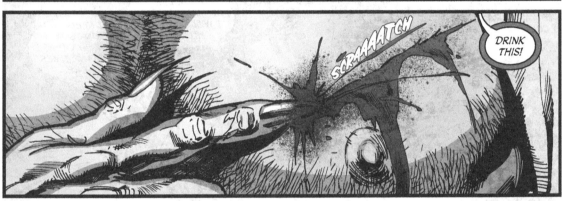

CHAPTER TWENTY-TWO

Jonathan Harker's Journal

October 3

*Van Helsing and Seward found Renfield dead on the floor. The **attendant** admitted he fell asleep. But he did remember hearing Renfield calling out "God!" several times.*

WE MUST BE HONEST AND OPEN WITH EACH OTHER. BESIDES, NOTHING CAN BE MORE PAINFUL THAT WHAT I HAVE ALREADY GONE THROUGH.

YOU ARE NOT AFRAID OF WHAT MIGHT HAPPEN TO YOU?

NO. I WOULD KILL MYSELF BEFORE I HARM OTHERS.

YOU MUST NOT THINK OF THAT. YOU MUST NOT DIE UNTIL COUNT DRACULA IS TRULY DEAD. OTHERWISE YOU WILL BECOME LIKE HIM.

YOU HAVE TO LIVE!

IF I AM SUPPOSED TO LIVE, I WILL TRY TO DO SO.

IT IS GOOD THAT WE DID NOT DO ANYTHING WITH THE BOXES NEXT DOOR AT CARFAX. COUNT DRACULA DOES NOT KNOW OUR PLAN.

WE HAVE UNTIL THE SUN SETS TO HUNT DOWN ALL THE BOXES AND **CLEANSE** THEM.

WE ARE WASTING TIME. WE NEED TO BREAK INTO THAT HOUSE IN PICCADILLY.

WHAT ABOUT THE POLICE?

WE WILL GO AFTER TEN. WE WILL GET A **LOCKSMITH** AND PRETEND THAT WE ARE LOCKED OUT OF OUR OWN HOUSE.

*We decided to **destroy** the boxes at Carfax right away.*

NOW, MY FRIENDS, OUR ADVENTURE BEGINS. MADAM MINA, YOU WILL BE SAFE HERE UNTIL SUNSET. IF WE ARE GOING TO RETURN, WE WILL RETURN BEFORE THEN.

FIRST, LET ME GIVE YOU SOMETHING TO PROTECT YOURSELF.

I TOUCH YOUR FOREHEAD WITH THIS PIECE OF HOLY WAFER –

AAAHH!

THIS MARK WILL STAY ON YOUR FOREHEAD UNTIL WE BEAT OUR ENEMY.

Van Helsing's words were full of hope.

We entered the old *chapel* just like we did before. Nothing had changed.

WE MUST CLEANSE THIS DIRT AND MAKE IT HOLY.

We laid a *holy wafer* in each box and secured the lids. Then we went to *Piccadilly*.

Arthur found a *locksmith*. We entered the house without any trouble.

There were only eight boxes – one was missing. We opened and *cleansed* each of the eight boxes with *holy wafers*.

CHAPTER TWENTY-THREE

Searching through the house we found the two addresses where boxes had been delivered, along with keys to get in.

Arthur and Quincey went off to *destroy* them.

Dr. Seward's Diary
October 3
Harker is miserable. He has aged overnight. His hair has turned white because of his sadness.

But, he still has a lot of energy.

We were surprised by a knock at the door. It was a *telegram* from Mina:

"DRACULA HAS JUST LEFT CARFAX. HE IS ON HIS WAY THERE."

THANK GOODNESS WE WILL MEET SOON. ALL I WANT TO DO IS WIPE THIS MONSTER FROM THE FACE OF THE EARTH.

I WOULD SELL MY *SOUL* TO DO IT.

115

Arthur and Quincey returned.

WE FOUND BOTH PLACES AND DESTROYED ALL TWELVE BOXES.

NOW WE HAVE TO WAIT HERE FOR COUNT DRACULA. WE CANNOT WAIT TOO LONG. WE DON'T WANT TO LEAVE MRS. HARKER ALONE AFTER SUNSET.

HE WILL BE HERE SOON ENOUGH.

We heard a key at the front door.

chchik

Quiet! Get ready!

We got into position.

clump clump

The slow footsteps came closer.

Count Dracula seemed to know something was wrong.

Before we could do anything, he flew right past us into the room.

He was as quick as a **panther**.

We had no plan of attack and did not know what to do.

Harker went to attack him, but Count Dracula was too fast.

swiiijsh

Count Dracula looked like he was going to kill Harker.

As I held out my **crucifix**, I felt a power fly through my arm.

YOU THINK YOU ARE SMARTER THAN I AM.

YOU THINK YOU HAVE LEFT ME WITHOUT A PLACE TO REST. BUT I HAVE MORE. MY **REVENGE** HAS ONLY JUST BEGUN!

BAH!

SKAAAAAAAAASH

THE GIRLS YOU LOVE ARE ALREADY MINE.

THEY ARE MY CREATURES! THEY WILL DO WHATEVER I TELL THEM TO DO!

FOLLOW HIM!

When they got outside, there was no sign of Count Dracula.

WE CANNOT DO ANYTHING ELSE HERE. LET'S GO BACK TO PROTECT MADAM MINA.

WE SHOULD NOT BE TOO DOWN ON OURSELVES. ONLY ONE BOX IS LEFT. WE HAVE TO FIND IT.

We went home with sad hearts.

Jonathan Harker's Journal
October 4, Morning

JONATHAN, REMEMBER THAT THIS IS NOT AN ACT OF HATE. THE MONSTER WHO CAUSES THIS MISERY IS THE SADDEST OF US ALL. WE SHOULD HAVE SOME PITY FOR HIM.

I WOULD DO ANYTHING TO KILL HIM FOREVER.

PLEASE, NO. ONE DAY, I MYSELF MIGHT NEED SUCH PITY FROM YOU.

119

I HAVE AN IDEA. VAN HELSING HAS TO **HYPNOTIZE** ME, AND THEN MAYBE I CAN GIVE YOU INFORMATION.

GET HIM QUICKLY!

WHERE ARE YOU?

I DO NOT KNOW. EVERYTHING IS DARK.

WHAT DO YOU HEAR?

I HEAR MOVING WATER. SMALL WAVES.

ARE YOU ON A SHIP?

YES! I CAN HEAR **CREWMEN** AND CHAINS.

Van Helsing stopped, and Mina woke up.

IT IS NOT TOO LATE. COUNT DRACULA IS IN THE LAST BOX AND HAS ESCAPED FROM LONDON ON A SHIP.

LET'S FOLLOW HIM!

CHAPTER TWENTY-FOUR

October 5

OUR **ENEMY** IS GOING BACK TO HIS CASTLE IN TRANSYLVANIA. I AM SURE HE WILL SAIL THROUGH THE BLACK SEA.

WE FOUND ONLY ONE SHIP HEADED THAT WAY — *THE CZARINA CATHERINE.*

WHEN WE ASKED ABOUT IT, WE WERE TOLD THAT A TALL MAN, THIN AND PALE, GAVE SPECIFIC INSTRUCTIONS ABOUT A BOX.

SO OUR **ENEMY** IS AT SEA, WITH THE FOG AT HIS **COMMAND.**

Dr. Seward's Diary
October 12
Mrs. Harker was in a serious mood ...

CHAPTER TWENTY-FIVE

IT IS IMPORTANT TO REMEMBER THAT I AM DIFFERENT FROM YOU. MY BLOOD IS **POISONED**, AND MY **SOUL** IS UNDER ATTACK. SHOULD THE TIME COME, YOU MUST PROMISE ME THAT YOU WILL KILL ME.

WHEN WILL THAT BE?

WHEN I AM SO EVIL THAT IT WOULD BE BETTER FOR ME TO DIE THAN TO LIVE.

YOU WILL DRIVE A **STAKE** THROUGH MY HEART AND CUT OFF MY HEAD.

I GIVE YOU MY WORD.

MY TRUE FRIEND!

MY WORD, ALSO.

AND I!

ME, TOO.

DO I HAVE TO MAKE THAT PROMISE TO MY OWN WIFE?

YOU MOST OF ALL. OUR **SOULS** WILL BE TOGETHER FOREVER.

Jonathan Harker's Journal
October 15, Varna
We traveled night and day. We arrived in Varna at five o'clock.

Mina is well and seems to be getting stronger. Van Helsing **hypnotizes** her at sunrise and sunset. It appears that Count Dracula is still at sea.

We plan to **board** the ship as soon as it arrives.

Even if Count Dracula turns into a bat, he cannot travel over running water without help. He will not be able to leave the ship.

People would notice if he suddenly appeared as a man, so he has to stay in his box.

We can surprise him and make him truly dead, just as we did for Lucy, before he wakes up.

We should not have much trouble with the **officials** here. We have plenty of money to **bribe** them with!

October 16
Mina still hears waves.

We have arranged for the **officials** to tell us when the ship is getting close to Varna.

Dr. Seward's Diary
October 24
A week of waiting. We have been told that the ship has been seen and will be here tomorrow morning.

October 25
No more news of the ship.

October 26.
Still nothing.

October 27
No news of the ship. Mrs. Harker reported the usual.

I still hear water, but the waves are quieter.

LET'S GET ORGANIZED. ARTHUR, GET THE TRAIN TICKETS FOR US TO GO TO GALATZ TOMORROW.

JONATHAN, ARRANGE FOR US TO **BOARD** THE SHIP.

QUINCEY, GET OUR TRAVELING PAPERS.

While Mina was **hypnotized**, Count Dracula was able to read her mind. He found out that we were waiting for him and he escaped.

Mina did not know Count Dracula was doing this. We should not tell her.

We are in a lot of danger.

We must trust in God.

CHAPTER TWENTY-SIX

Dr. Seward's Diary
October 29
Last night, at
sunset ...

It is still. I do not hear waves, just some water swirling by the ship.

What is this?

I see light, and I can feel air on my face.

She suddenly opened her eyes.

WOULD ANYONE LIKE TEA? YOU MUST ALL BE SO TIRED!

COUNT DRACULA IS CLOSE TO LAND. HE HAS LEFT HIS BOX, BUT HE IS NOT ON SHORE.

AT NIGHT HE CAN CHANGE HIS SHAPE AND JUMP ON SHORE, AS HE DID IN WHITBY.

BUT IN THE DAY HE CAN ONLY ESCAPE IF SOMEONE CARRIES HIM.

IF HE DOESN'T ESCAPE TO SHORE TONIGHT, WE MAY ARRIVE IN TIME.

It is in this **spirit** of hope that we travel toward Galatz.

October 30,
Morning
We are near
Galatz.

It is dark. I hear men talking in a strange language and water **lapping** very close to me. Wood is creaking, and I can hear cattle in the distance.

Galatz

Mina Harker's Journal
October 30
Mr. Morris took me to our hotel while the others went about their **business**.

Jonathan Harker's Journal
October 30
On **board** *The Czarina Catherine* with Captain Donelson ...

WE TRAVELED IN FOG THE WHOLE TIME.

SOME OF THE **CREW** WERE NERVOUS ABOUT A **BOX** THAT A STRANGE MAN HAD PUT ON **BOARD** THE SHIP IN LONDON.

THEY WANTED TO THROW IT **OVERBOARD**!

WHEN THE FOG FINALLY DISAPPEARED, WE DISCOVERED THAT WE WERE IN GALATZ.

THE **CREW** STILL WANTED TO THROW THE BOX **OVERBOARD**, BUT I TALKED THEM OUT OF IT.

IN THE MORNING, A MAN CAME TO CLAIM THE BOX FOR COUNT DRACULA. I WAS HAPPY TO GET RID OF IT.

Later, we met the man who claimed the box. It was handed over to someone called Petrof Skinsky. He worked with some *traders*.

When we tried to find him, we were told that his body had been found dead in a graveyard.

His throat had been torn open by some wild animal.

Mina Harker's Journal
October 30, Evening
The men came back to the hotel tired and unhappy.

After they rested, I gathered them together.

I BELIEVE THAT COUNT DRACULA CAME OUT OF HIS BOX WHEN IT WAS ON LAND. HE MET WITH SKINSKY TO GIVE INSTRUCTIONS FOR THE BOX.

SKINSKY WAS TOLD TO SEND THE BOX UP SOME RIVER IN AN OPEN BOAT. ONCE THAT WAS ARRANGED, COUNT DRACULA **MURDERED** SKINSKY TO COVER HIS TRACKS.

LOOK AT THIS MAP. THE RIVER SERETH IS GOOD FOR THE **TRADERS** TO USE BECAUSE IT RUNS NEAR COUNT DRACULA'S CASTLE.

Mina Harker's Journal
October 30, Later

We cannot trust anyone, so we will drive ourselves.

We are all armed. I cannot carry a **crucifix**, but everyone else has one. It took all my **courage** to say good-bye to Jonathan.

We may never see each other again.

Jonathan Harker's Journal
October 30, Night
Thank goodness Arthur knows how to control this boat.

It seems to be getting colder as we rush into this dark and scary world.

Dr. Seward's Diary
November 2
Three days on the road. We are tired, but we must keep going.

November 4
Arthur's boat had an accident in some rough waters. The **traders** know the river better than we do. Arthur was able to fix the boat.

CHAPTER TWENTY-SEVEN

Mina Harker's Journal
November 2, Night
We drove all day. The country gets wilder the farther we go into it.

Note written by Abraham Van Helsing
November 4
This is to my old friend, Jack Seward.
The cold seems to have affected Madam Mina. She sleeps all the time!
While **hypnotized**, she said that Count Dracula was in darkness and she could hear water swirling.

IF SHE IS GOING TO SLEEP ALL DAY, THEN I WILL NOT SLEEP AT NIGHT.

November 5, Morning
The farther we go, the wilder it gets.

I made a fire before it got too dark.

Then I drew a large circle around us and placed a crumbled **holy wafer** in it. Madam Mina could not cross the circle, which meant that none of those we feared could either.

The horses were nervous and I had to calm them down. In the snow and **mist**, I saw those women who tried to attack Jonathan.

I called to Madam Mina:

YOU ARE SAFE HERE.

DO NOT WORRY ABOUT ME! I AM PROTECTED FROM THEM. THEY CANNOT HARM ME!

At least I have not lost my mind.

I left Madam Mina asleep in the circle and went to the castle. Jonathan's journal helped me get here.

I found my way to the old **chapel**. The air smelled so bad it made me dizzy.

I knew there were at least three graves to find.

I found the first one.

She lay in her **vampire** sleep, beautiful and full of life.

I seemed under a kind of **spell** and could not move; but I snapped out of it to do my work.

AAAIEEEGH

It was terrible, but it is done.

Before I left the castle, I fixed its doors so that Count Dracula cannot enter.

Madam Mina woke up when I returned.

LET'S LEAVE HERE AND GO MEET MY HUSBAND. I FEEL HIM CLOSE BY.

The poor **souls**. Once my knife cut off their heads, their bodies crumbled to dust.

And so we head east to meet our friends – and Count Dracula, whom Madam Mina says is on his way.

Mina Harker's Journal
November 6
I was tired after a mile of walking. We could hear wolves, so Van Helsing looked for shelter.

He found a perfect place.

WE WILL BE SAFE HERE.

LOOK! MADAM MINA, LOOK!

There was a group of men with a cart carrying a large chest.

It was getting late. It would soon be night, when Count Dracula can take on a new shape.

I CAN SEE TWO HORSEMEN. IT MUST BE QUINCEY AND JACK.

Looking around I saw two more men. It was Jonathan and Arthur.

STOP!

STOP!

The leader gave an order, and his men prepared to shoot their guns.

All four of our men **raced** to the cart. Jonathan and Quincey were determined to finish before the sun set.

BLAM

THOK

Jonathan was brave.

Soon, he was on top of the cart.

THWAK

With amazing strength ...

GNNYAAGH!

THUD

... he threw it to the ground.

SHLK

All this time, Quincey fought bravely.

He seemed unharmed ...

URLLLGHHHH!

... but when he went to Jonathan, I could see that he was hurt.

SCREEEECH!

They tried to open the box.

BLAM

The other men knew they were defeated, and they ran away.

The top of the chest was opened.

KLOOF

I saw Count Dracula lying on the dirt.

He was very **pale**, but his red eyes **glared** with the look I knew only too well.

He saw that the sun was setting, and he looked like he had won.

139

Jonathan *immediately* used his knife.

HAUULLGGH!

SHLKK

Quincey's knife plunged into the heart.

GULGH!

SKTCH

AAARRGGHHH!

It was like a miracle. Before our very eyes ...

... the whole body crumbled into dust ...

... and disappeared.

In his final moments, he had a look of absolute peace.

Quincey fell to the ground.

QUINCEY!

SEVEN YEARS AGO WE WENT THROUGH SOME OF THE WORST TIMES WE HAD EVER SEEN. THE JOY WE HAVE KNOWN SINCE THEN WAS WORTH ALL THE PAIN.

WE LOOK BACK AT THE PAST WITHOUT SADNESS. ARTHUR AND JACK ARE BOTH HAPPILY MARRIED.

THE ONLY EVIDENCE WE HAVE OF WHAT HAPPENED IS A STACK OF TYPED-OUT JOURNALS AND NOTEBOOKS.

HOW COULD WE EXPECT ANYONE TO BELIEVE US?

MINA BELIEVES THAT HE SHARES SOME OF OUR FRIEND'S BRAVERY.

OUR SON'S BIRTHDAY IS THE SAME DAY THAT QUINCEY MORRIS DIED.

HIS NAME IS LONG AND INCLUDES MOST OF OUR NAMES, BUT WE CALL HIM QUINCEY.

WE DO NOT NEED ANYONE TO BELIEVE US!

THIS BOY WILL LEARN HOW BRAVE AND FEARLESS HIS MOTHER IS.

WHEN HE IS OLDER, HE WILL UNDERSTAND HOW MEN RISKED THEIR LIVES FOR HER.

In the summer, we made a journey to Transylvania and visited the old ground that held such terrible memories for us.

It was hard even for us to believe the things we had seen were true. There were no traces of any of it.

The castle stood high above a **wasteland**, just like it always did.

– Jonathan Harker

144

DRACULA

End

Glossary

A

analyze / ænəlaɪz / – (analyzes, analyzing, analyzed) (V) If you analyze something, you consider it carefully in order to fully understand it or to find out what it consists of.

attendant / ətɛndənt / – (attendants) (N) An attendant is someone whose job is to serve or help people.

Attila / ətɪlə / – (N) Attila was the King of the Huns from the year 434 AD until his death in 453 AD.

autopsy / ɔtɒpsi / – (autopsies) (N) An autopsy is an examination of a dead body by a doctor who cuts it open in order to try to discover the cause of death.

B

blood level / blʌd levəl / – (blood levels) (N) A blood level is the amount of blood inside of a person or animal.

board / bɔrd / – 1. (boards, boarding, boarded) (V) When you board a train, ship, or aircraft, you get on it in order to travel somewhere. 2. (V) When you are on board a train, ship, or aircraft, you are on it or in it.

bribe / braɪb / – (bribes, bribing, bribed) (V) If one person bribes another, they give him or her a sum of money or something valuable in order to persuade him or her to do something.

business / bɪznɪs / – 1. (businesses) (N) Business is work relating to the production, buying, and selling of goods or services. 2. (businesses) (N) You can use business to refer in a general way to an event, situation, or activity.

C

case / keɪs / – (cases) (N) A case is a particular situation or instance.

century / sɛntʃəri / – (centuries) (N) A century is any period of a hundred years.

chapel / tʃæpᵊl / – (chapels) (N) A chapel is a small church in or attached to a building.

charm / tʃɑrm / – (charms) (N) A charm is an act, saying, or object that is believed to have magic powers.

cleanse / klɛnz / – (cleanses, cleansing, cleansed) (V) To cleanse a place, person, or organization of something dirty, unpleasant, or evil means to make them free from it.

coach / koʊtʃ / – (coaches) (N) A coach is an enclosed vehicle with four wheels which is pulled by horses, and in which people used to travel.

coast guard / koʊst gɑrd / – (N) A coast guard is a person whose job is to be responsible for the safety and what goes on in a section of water and its coast.

command / kəmænd / – (commands, commanding, commanded) (V) If someone in authority commands you to do something, they tell you that you must do it.

companion / kəmpænyən / – (companions) (N) A companion is someone who you spend time with or who you are traveling with.

confident / kɒnfɪdənt / – (ADJ) If you are confident about something, you are certain that it will happen in the way you want it to.

courage / kɜrɪdʒ / – (N) Courage is the quality shown by someone who does something difficult or dangerous, even though he or she may be afraid.

courtyard / kɔrtyard / – (courtyards) (N) A courtyard is an open area of ground which is surrounded by buildings or walls.

cover his tracks / kʌvər hɪz træks / – (PHRASE) If you cover your tracks, you hide anything that shows where you have been or what you have done so that no one can find or catch you.

crew / kru / – (crews) (N) The crew of a ship, an aircraft, or a spacecraft is the people who work on and operate it.

crewman / krumæn / – (crewmen) (N) A crewman is a member of a crew on a ship.

crucifix / krusɪfɪks / – (crucifixes) (N) A crucifix is a small figure of Christ on the cross.

culture / kʌltʃər / – (cultures) (N) A culture is a particular society or civilization, especially considered in relation to its beliefs, way of life, or art.

cure / kyʊər / – 1. (cures, curing, cured) (V) If doctors or medical treatments cure someone or cure an illness or injury, they make the person well again. 2. (cures) (N) A cure for an illness is a medicine or other treatment that cures the illness.

D

defeat / dɪfit / – (defeats, defeating, defeated) (V) If you defeat someone, you win a victory over them in a battle, game, or contest.

depressed / dɪprɛst / – (ADJ) If you are depressed, you are sad and feel that you cannot enjoy anything.

descended / dɪsɛndɪd / – (ADJ) A person who is descended from someone who lived a long time ago is directly related to them.

description / dɪskrɪpʃᵊn / – (descriptions) (N) A description of someone or something is an account which explains what they are or what they look like.

desert / dɪzɜrt / – (deserts, deserting, deserted) (V) If people or animals desert a place, they leave it and it becomes empty.

destroy / dɪstrɔɪ / – (destroys, destroying, destroyed) (V) To destroy something means to cause so much damage to it that it is completely ruined or does not exist any more.

doom / dum / – [N] Doom is a terrible future state or event which you cannot prevent.

duty / duti / – [N] If you say that something is your duty, you believe that you ought to do it because it is your responsibility.

E

enclose / ɪnklouz / – (encloses, enclosing, enclosed) [V] If a place or object is enclosed by something, the place or object is inside that thing or completely surrounded by it.

enemy / ɛnəmi / – (enemies) [N] If someone is your enemy, that person hates you or wants to harm you.

estate / ɪsteɪt / – (estates) [N] An estate is a large area of land in the country which is owned by a person, family, or organization.

exhaust / ɪgzɔst / – (exhausts, exhausting, exhausted) [V] If something exhausts you, it makes you very tired.

F

facedown / feɪs daʊn / – [ADV] If someone is lying facedown, they are lying with their face turned down to the ground or floor.

faithful / feɪθfəl / – [ADJ] Someone who is faithful to a person, organization, or idea remains firm in their support for them.

famine / fæmɪn / – (famines) [N] Famine is a situation in which large numbers of people have little or no food, and many of them die.

fascinate / fæsɪneɪt / – (fascinates, fascinating, fascinated) [V] If something fascinates you, you find it extremely interesting.

favor / feɪvər / – (favors) [N] If you do someone a favor, you do something to help them even though you do not have to.

fiancé / fiɑnseɪ / – (fiancés) [N] A person's fiance is the person to whom they are engaged to be married.

fierce / fɪərs / – (fiercer, fiercest) [ADJ] A fierce animal or person is very aggressive or angry.

forbid / fərbɪd / – (forbids, forbidding, forbade, forbidden) [V] If you forbid someone to do something, or if you forbid an activity, you order that it must not be done.

fortune / fɔrtʃən / – (fortunes) [N] You can refer to a large sum of money as a fortune or a small fortune to emphasize how large it is.

fracture / fræktʃər / – (fractures, fracturing, fractured) [V] If something such as a bone is fractured or fractures, it gets a crack or break in it.

funeral arrangements / fyunərəl əreɪndʒmənts / – [N] Funeral arrangements are the plans for a funeral, such as the time and location.

G

garlic / gɑrlɪk / – [N] Garlic is a small, white, round bulb. It has a strong flavor and is used in cooking.

glare / glɛər / – (glares, glaring, glared) [V] If you glare at someone, you look at them with an angry expression on your face.

grieve / griv / – (grieves, grieving, grieved) [V] If you grieve over something, especially someone's death, you feel very sad about it.

H

harbor / hɑrbər / – (harbors, harboring, harbored) [N] A harbor is an area of water which is partly enclosed by land or strong walls, so that boats can be left there safely.

hitch / hɪtʃ / – (hitches, hitching, hitched) [V] If you get hitched with someone, you marry them. This is a slang word for getting married.

holy / houli / – (holier, holiest) [ADJ] Something that is holy is considered to be special because it is connected with God or a particular religion.

horror / hɔrər / – (horrors) [N] Horror is a feeling of great shock, fear, and worry caused by something extremely unpleasant.

hospitality / hɒspɪtælɪti / – [N] Hospitality is friendly, welcoming behavior toward guests or people you have just met.

humanity / hyumænɪti / – (humanities) [N] All the people in the world can be referred to as humanity.

Huns / hʌns / – [N] The Huns were a group of nomadic central Asian people, who gained control of a large part of central and eastern Europe under Attila.

hypnotize / hɪpnətaɪz / – (hypnotizes, hypnotizing, hypnotized) [V] If someone hypnotizes you, they put you into a state in which you seem to be asleep but can still see, hear, or respond to things said to you.

I

identical / aɪdɛntɪkəl / – [ADJ] Things that are identical are exactly the same.

ignore / ɪgnɔr / – (ignores, ignoring, ignored) [V] If you ignore someone or something, you pay no attention to them.

immediately / ɪmidiɪtli / – [ADV] If something happens immediately, it happens without any delay.

insane / ɪnseɪn / – [ADJ] Someone who is insane is severely mentally ill.

insane asylum / ɪnseɪn əsaɪləm / – [N] An insane asylum is what mental hospitals used to be called. It is a place where people who are severely mentally ill are cared for.

intrigue / ɪntrig / – (intrigues, intriguing, intrigued) [V] If something, especially something strange, intrigues you, it interests you and you want to know more about it.

invisible / ɪnvɪzɪbəl / – [ADJ] If something is invisible, you cannot see it, for example, because it is transparent, hidden, or very small.

L

lair / lər / – [N] A lair is a place of safety or a place for hiding.

lap / læp / – (laps, lapping, lapped) (V) When water laps against something such as the shore or the side of a boat, it touches it gently and makes a soft sound.

legend / lɛdʒᵊnd / – (legends) (N) A legend is a very old and popular story that may be true.

locksmith / lɒksmɪθ / – (locksmiths) (N) A locksmith is a person whose job is to make or repair locks.

lord / lɔrd / – (lords) (N) A lord is a man who has a high rank in the nobility, for example, an earl, a viscount, or a marquis.

M

miserable / mɪzərəbᵊl / – (ADJ) If you are miserable, you are very unhappy.

mist / mɪst / – (mists) (N) Mist consists of a large number of tiny drops of water in the air, which make it difficult to see very far.

mortal life / mɔrtᵊl laɪf / – (ADJ) If you refer to the fact that someone has a mortal life, you mean that they have to die and cannot live forever.

mourn / mɔrn / – (mourns, mourning, mourned) (V) If you mourn someone who has died or mourn for them, you are very sad that they have died and show your sorrow in the way that you behave.

murder / mɜrdər / – 1. (murders) (N) Murder is the crime of deliberately killing a person. 2. (murders, murdering, murdered) (V) To murder someone means to commit the crime of killing a person deliberately.

N

nationality / næʃənælɪti / – (nationalities) (N) If you have the nationality of a particular country, you were born there or have the legal right to be a citizen.

newspaper clipping / nuzpeɪpər klɪpɪŋ / – (newspaper clippings) (N) A newspaper clipping is an article, picture, or advertisement that has been cut from a newspaper.

noble / noʊbᵊl / – (nobler, noblest) (ADJ) If you say that someone is a noble person, you admire and respect them because they are unselfish and morally good.

nonsense / nɒnsɛns / – (N) If you say that something spoken or written is nonsense, you think it is untrue or silly.

O

official / əfɪʃᵊl / – (officials) (N) An official is a person who holds a position of authority in an organization.

operate / ɒpəreɪt / – (operates, operating, operated) (V) When surgeons operate on a patient, they cut open the patient's body in order to remove, replace, or repair a diseased or damaged part.

operation / ɒpəreɪʃᵊn / – (operations) (N) When a patient has an operation, a surgeon cuts open their body in order to remove, replace, or repair a diseased or damaged part.

overboard / oʊvərbɔrd / – (ADV) If you fall overboard, you fall over the side of a boat into the water.

P

pale / peɪl / – (paler, palest) (ADJ) If someone looks pale, their face looks a lighter color than usual, usually because they are ill, frightened, or shocked.

panther / pænθər / – (panthers) (N) A panther is a large, black wildcat.

paralyze / pærəlaɪz / – (paralyzes, paralyzing, paralyzed) (V) If someone is paralyzed by an accident or an illness, they have no feeling in their body, or in part of their body, and are unable to move.

peasant / pɛzᵊnt / – (peasants) (N) People refer to small farmers or farm workers in poor countries as peasants.

phonograph / foʊnəræf / – (phonographs) (N) A phonograph is an old-fashioned record player or recorder.

Piccadilly / pɪkadɪli / – (N) Piccadilly is a major street in central London in the United Kingdom.

pierce / pɪərs / – (pierces, piercing, pierced) (V) If a sharp object pierces something, or if you pierce something with a sharp object, the object goes into it and makes a hole in it.

poison / pɔɪzᵊn / – (poisons, poisoning, poisoned) (V) To poison someone or something means to harm or damage them by giving them poison or putting poison into them.

precious / prɛʃəs / – (ADJ) If something such as a resource is precious, it is valuable and should not be wasted or used badly.

propose / prəpoʊz / – (proposes, proposing, proposed) (V) If you propose to someone, or propose marriage to them, you ask them to marry you.

proposal / prəpoʊzᵊl / – (proposals) (N) A proposal is the act of asking someone to marry you.

R

race / reɪs / – 1. (races) (N) A race is one of the major groups which human beings can be divided into according to their physical features, such as the color of their skin. 2. (races, racing, raced) (V) If you race somewhere, you go there as quickly as possible.

record / rɛkərd / – 1. (records) (N) If you keep a record of something, you keep a written account or photographs of it so that it can be referred to later. 2. (records, recording, recorded) (V) If you record something such as a speech or performance, you put it on tape or film so that it can be heard or seen again later.

recording / rɪkɔrdɪŋ / – (recordings) (N) A recording of something is a record, CD, tape, video, or DVD of it.

reject / rɪdʒɛkt / – (rejects, rejecting, rejected, rejection) (V) If you reject something such as a proposal or a request, you do not accept it or agree to it.

relax / rɪlæks / – (relaxes, relaxing, relaxed) (V) If you relax or if something relaxes you, you feel more calm and less worried or tense.

remarkable / rɪmɑrkəbᵊl / – (ADJ) Someone or something that is remarkable is very impressive or unusual.

remove / rɪmuv / – (removes, removing, removed) (V) If you remove something from a place, you take it away.

reservation / rɛzərveɪʃᵊn / – (reservations) [N] If you make a reservation, you arrange for something such as a table in a restaurant or a room in a hotel to be kept for you.

responsible / rɪspɒnsɪbᵊl / – [ADJ] If someone or something is responsible for a particular event or situation, they are the cause of it or they can be blamed for it.

revenge / rɪvɛndʒ / – [N] Revenge involves hurting or punishing someone who has hurt or harmed you.

rise / raɪz / – (rises, rising, rose) [V] If something rises, it moves upward.

rumor / rumər / – (rumors) [N] A rumor is a story or piece of information that may or may not be true, but that people are talking about.

S

sane / seɪn / – (saner, sanest) [ADJ] Someone who is sane is able to think and behave normally and reasonably, and is not mentally ill.

satan / seɪtᵊn / – [N] In religions such as Christianity and Islam, Satan is the devil, a powerful evil being who is the chief opponent of God.

scenery / sinəri / – [N] The scenery in a country area is the land, water, or plants that you can see around you.

scold / skoʊld / – (scolds, scolding, scolded) [V] If you scold someone, you speak angrily to them because they have done something wrong.

seal / sil / – (seals, sealing, sealed) [V] If you seal something, you make it definite and final.

shipment / ʃɪpmənt / – (shipments) [N] A shipment is an amount of a particular kind of cargo that is sent to another country on a ship, train, airplane, or other vehicle.

shorthand / ʃɔrthænd / – [N] Shorthand is a quick way of writing and uses signs to represent words or syllables.

shudder / ʃʌdər / – (shudders, shuddering, shuddered) [V] If you shudder, you shake with fear, horror, or disgust, or because you are cold.

situation / sɪtʃueɪʃᵊn / – (situations) [N] You use situation to refer generally to what is happening in a particular place at a particular time, or to refer to what is happening to you.

skeptical / skɛptɪkᵊl / – [ADJ] If you are skeptical about something, you have doubts about it.

sleepwalk / slipwɔk / – (sleepwalks, sleepwalking, sleepwalked) [V] If you sleepwalk, you walk around while you are asleep.

soul / soʊl / – (souls) [N] Your soul is the part of you that consists of your mind, character, thoughts, and feelings. Many people believe that your soul continues existing after your body is dead.

source / sɔrs / – (sources) [N] The source of something is the person, place, or thing which you get it from.

specific / spɪsɪfɪk / – 1. [ADJ] You use specific to refer to a particular exact area, problem, or subject. 2. [ADJ] If someone is specific, they give a description that is precise and exact. You can also use specific to describe their description.

spell / spɛl / – (spells) [N] A spell is a situation in which events are controlled by a magical power.

spirit / spɪrɪt / – 1. [N] A spirit is a ghost or supernatural being. 2. [N] The spirit in which you do something is the attitude you have when you are doing it.

stake / steɪk / – (stakes) [N] A stake is a pointed wooden post.

struggle / strʌgᵊl / – (struggles, struggling, struggled) [V] If you struggle to do something difficult, you try hard to do it.

study / stʌdi / – [N] A study is a room in a house which is used for reading, writing, and studying.

surgical / sɜrdʒɪkᵊl / – [ADJ] Surgical equipment and clothing is used in surgery.

sympathy / sɪmpəθi / – (sympathies) [N] If you have sympathy for someone who is in a bad situation, you are sorry for them, and show this in the way you behave toward them.

Szekelys / sekɛls / – [N] The Szekelys are a subgroup of the Hungarian people who live in the Transylvania region of Romania.

T

take all the credit / teɪk ɔl ðə krɛdɪt / – [PHRASE] If you take all the credit, you accept all of the praise for an action or project.

tame / teɪm / – 1. (tames, taming, tamed, tamer, tamest) [ADJ] A tame animal or bird is not afraid of humans. 2. (tames, taming, tamed, tamer, tamest) [V] If someone tames a wild animal or bird, they train it not to be afraid of humans.

telegram / tɛlɪgræm / – (telegrams) [N] A telegram is a message that is sent by telegraph and then printed and delivered to someone.

tomb / tum / – (tombs) [N] A tomb is a stone structure containing the body of a dead person.

track / træk / – (tracks, tracking, tracked) [V] If you track something, you try to find it by following signs.

trader / treɪdər / – (traders) [N] A trader is a person whose job is to trade in goods.

trance / træns / – (trances) [N] If someone is in a trance, they seem to be asleep, but they still have their eyes open and can see and hear things.

transfusion / trænsfyuʒᵊn / – (transfusions) [N] A blood transfusion is a process in which blood is injected into the body of a person who is sick or badly injured.

treasure / trɛʒər / – (treasures, treasuring, treasured) [N] Treasure is a collection of valuable old objects, such as gold coins and jewels.

treatment / tritmənt / – (treatments) [N] Treatment is medical attention given to a sick or injured person or animal.

typewriter / taɪpraɪtər / – (typewriters) [N] A typewriter is a machine with keys which are pressed in order to print letters, numbers, or other characters onto paper.

U

upset / ʌpsɛt / — (upsets, upsetting, upset) (V) If something upsets you, it makes you feel worried or unhappy.

urgent / ɜrdʒ°nt / — (ADJ) If something is urgent, it needs to be dealt with as soon as possible.

V

vampire / væmpaɪər / — (vampires) (N) In horror stories, vampires are creatures that come out of graves at night and suck the blood of living people.

W

wafer / weɪfər / — (wafers) (N) A wafer is a thin, crisp cookie that can have religious meaning.

wasteland / weɪstlænd / — (wastelands) (N) A wasteland is an area of land on which not much can grow or which has been spoiled in some way

wheel / wil / — (wheels, wheeling, wheeled) (N) The wheel of a ship or other vehicle is the circular object that is used to steer it.

worship / wɜrʃɪp / — (worships, worshipping, worshipped) (V) If you worship someone or something, you love them or admire them very much.

wound / wund / — (wounds) (N) A wound is damage to part of your body, especially a cut or a hole in your flesh, which is caused by a gun, knife, or other weapon.

Abraham "Bram" Stoker

[1847–1912]

Abraham Stoker was born on November 8, 1847 in Dublin, Ireland. He went by the name "Bram." As a child, he was often sick. He spent much of his time in bed until he was seven years old and started school. He spent a lot of his time reading and thinking. Even though he was a sick child, he grew up to become smart, strong, and athletic. He went to Trinity College in Dublin and studied math. He was an honor student from 1864 to 1870. While at college, he met the author and playwright Oscar Wilde. They both shared a love of literature and theater.

When Stoker left Trinity College, he worked for the government. He also wrote and became a theater critic for the *Dublin Evening Mail*. In December 1876, he attended the Theatre Royal in Dublin. He gave a good review of the play *Hamlet* by the actor Henry Irving. Irving invited Stoker to his hotel for dinner, and they became friends.

Stoker married Florence Balcombe in 1878, and they moved to London. Stoker became the manager of the Lyceum Theatre, which was owned by Irving. A year later, Florence gave birth to a boy, their only child. They named their son Irving.

Stoker was very busy between working as a theater manager and traveling with Irving. Stoker and Irving traveled a lot, including several visits to America. They were invited twice to the White House to meet President William McKinley and President Theodore Roosevelt.

Although he worked a lot, Stoker continued to write. He wrote four novels, two non-fiction works, and a collection of short stories between 1875 and 1895. In 1897, following years of research on European legends and history, *Dracula* was published. The writing style was different because it was presented as a collection of journals, records, and letters. This collection created a story that seemed strangely close to reality. The original manuscript for the book was thought to be lost. But in the 1980s, it was found in a barn in Pennsylvania. The manuscript had the working title of *The Un-Dead*. Because the name was changed right before the book was published, the first edition of *Dracula* had a poor-quality cover.

Even though today it is seen as the ultimate horror story,

Dracula did not receive good reviews when it was published. But, it sold well because vampire stories were popular at that time. Stoker published seven more novels after *Dracula*, but he was never a huge literary success. In fact, he had some very difficult times. The Lyceum Theatre got into financial trouble. And, a fire damaged part of the building and destroyed important scenery for plays. Irving sold the theatre in 1898. Stoker was no longer the manager. Stoker and Irving remained close friends.

Irving died in 1905. A year later, Stoker published *Personal Reminiscences of Henry Irving*. Stoker wrote more novels, but he had a few strokes that left him weak.

Bram Stoker died on April 20, 1912, the same week that *The Titanic* sank. None of Stoker's obituaries even mentioned his book *Dracula*.

Dracula movies
The story was first made into a movie in 1922. In order to avoid copyright issues, the filmmakers named it *Nosferatu*.

The character of Dracula became Count Orlock. Florence Stoker sued the filmmakers for stealing her late husband's work and won. The first official adaptation of *Dracula* was made in 1931. It starred Bela Lugosi as Dracula. The movie is still respected today, and was re-released in 1998 with new music by Philip Glass.

The Hammer Films version of 1958 is considered a classic. It starred Christopher Lee as Dracula, with Peter Cushing as Van Helsing. The movie was a huge success, and eight more Dracula-related movies followed. Christopher Lee became associated with the character. Lee appeared in a total of nine movies as Count Dracula. A more recent version of the story is *Bram Stoker's Dracula* (1992), directed by Francis Ford Coppola. Coppola added background elements, including Count Dracula's history before the story takes place. He also explained Dracula's obsession with England.

The Real Count Dracula
Stoker reveals that the fictional Count Dracula in the book was based on a real person when Van Helsing explains who their enemy is to the other characters (see page 95). Count Dracula was based on Vlad the Impaler, whose real name was Vlad Dracula. He is called Voivode Dracula in the story. Vlad Dracula was born in 1431 in Transylvania. He became the ruler of Wallachia, which is now Romania, in 1456. He was known for

being cruel. Not only would he kill his enemies, but he would have their bodies hung on wooden stakes. He did this as a warning to anyone thinking of challenging his leadership. During his reign, he had a grand castle built (Bran Castle, in the Carpathian Mountains). It was built using poor slaves. The slaves worked naked because they could not afford clothes. He is said to have once brutally killed the poor and needy people under his rule by gathering them in a large hall, locking the doors, and setting the building on fire. He would even have his own people tortured for his entertainment. He had a reputation for being very interested in blood and eating the flesh of his victims. Even though he was very cruel, he was respected and even admired. This is because he was very successful in battle and a good leader. He was eventually killed in battle against the Ottomans in 1476.

Although he was many things, Vlad Dracula was not a vampire. The name of Dracula was appealing to Stoker as it means "devil" in the language of Wallachia. Even though we cannot always separate legend from fact, Vlad Dracula was definitely evil-natured— much crueler than the noble, aristocratic character of Count Dracula. It is believed that Dracula's character was more inspired by Henry Irving's forceful character than by Vlad the Impaler's character.

Graphic Novel Creation

Here is a behind-the-scenes look at how *Dracula: The Graphic Novel* was made.

The Script

The first step in creating a graphic novel is making the script. The script is made by a writer. The writer looks at the original story written by Bram Stoker and then decides how the story will be told through pictures. The writer has to think about what each picture will look like, and write a description of it. Then the dialogue of the story is adapted for language learners. In the script below, you can see the original dialogue from the story in the left column, and the adapted dialogue in the right column.

PAGE 96

1. VAN HELSING is holding out his glass for HARKER to refresh it from the decanter as he continues.

VAN HELSING	And now we must settle what we do. We have here much data, and we must proceed to lay out our campaign. We know that from the castle to Whitby came fifty boxes of earth, all of which were delivered at Carfax; some of these boxes have been removed. We must trace each of these boxes; and when we are ready, we must either capture or kill this monster in his lair; or we must sterilise the earth, so that no more he can seek safety in it. We may find him in his form of man between the hours of noon and sunset, and so engage with him when he is at his most weak.	Now we have to plan our attack. We know that fifty boxes of dirt were delivered to Carfax. Some of these boxes have been removed. We must track each of these boxes. We must either kill this monster in his home, or we must make sure he cannot safely sleep in the dirt. Remember, he is weakest between noon and sunset when he is in the shape of a man.

2. VAN HELSING turns, smiling, to MINA, who is frowning at his words. HARKER, however, is relieved, placing a caring hand on her arm.

VAN HELSING	And now for you, Madam Mina, this night is the end until all be well. You are too precious to us to have such risk. When we part tonight, you no more must question. We shall act all the more free that you are not in the danger, such as we are.	Madam Mina, you are too precious. We cannot risk you getting hurt. We will be more willing to attack Count Dracula if we know you are not in any danger.

3. Close in on QUINCEY, as he is on his feet, fists clenched, his revolver drawn and in his hand, ready for action.

QUINCEY	As there is no time to lose, I vote we have a look in his house right now. Time is everything with him; and swift action on our part may save another victim.	We cannot waste any time. We should look in the house right away.

4. Suddenly, an ATTENDANT appears at the door to the asylum corridor. SEWARD is already on his feet by the door.

Caption (Seward)	Dr. Seward's Diary 1 October.– Just as we were about to leave . . .	Dr. Seward's Diary October 1 Just as we were about to leave . . .
ATTENDANT	Renfield wants to see you at once, Dr. Seward. I have never seen him so eager. If you don't see him soon, he will have one of his violent fits.	Renfield wants to see you right now, Dr. Seward.
SEWARD	All right; I'll go now.	I'll go now.
Arthur	May I come also?	May I come also?
QUINCEY	Me too?	Me, too?

Character Design

While the script is being written, the artist works on a design for each of the characters. Staz Johnson, the artist for *Dracula: The Graphic Novel*, wanted to represent the characters as they are described in Stoker's story. He did not want to be influenced by the way these famous characters have appeared in the many movie versions of the story.

Here you see some of his initial sketches for Count Dracula.

Here are some more sketches of other characters:

The Pencil Stage

The artist then reads the script and draws each page. This is the most difficult stage in the process because it involves turning a blank sheet of paper into art. The artist must consider many things during this stage, including the pacing of the story, body language of characters, character size, perspective, lettering space, texture, and lighting.

The Inking Stage

Next, texture and shadows are added to the illustrations. This is done by using black ink to fill in the shaded areas. This stage makes the pencil drawings sharper and more dramatic.

The Coloring Stage

The next stage really brings the illustrations to life. Color is added to the illustrations not only to fill the white space, but to add a 3D look to it. The skin tones in the characters' faces and the shadows in their hair help make them look like real people. Also, the shading on the walls and the light shining in the scene add to how realistic it looks.

Lettering

The last step is to add the captions, speech bubbles, and sound effects from the script. These words have to be added to the illustrations in a way that will be easy for the reader's eye to follow. If it is done well, the reader will have no problem following the dialogue from illustration to illustration. Once this is done, it is printed and made into a book.

Notes

OTHER CLASSICAL COMICS TITLES:

Henry V   1-4240-2877-9

Frankenstein   1-4240-3184-2

Great Expectations   1-4240-2882-5

Macbeth   1-4240-2873-6

Jane Eyre   1-4240-2887-6

A Christmas Carol   1-4240-4287-9

Romeo and Juliet   1-4240-4291-7

The Tempest   1-4240-4296-8

The Canterville Ghost
1-4240-4299-2

A Midsummer Night's Dream
1-111-83845-3

Wuthering Heights
1-111-83885-2